SPIRIT FOR CHANGE

Christopher Titmuss was a journalist in London, Turkey, Laos and Australia; in 1970 he became a Buddhist monk and spent the following six years in Thailand and India. He now teaches engaged spirituality and insight meditation around the world. He is a co-founder of a number of spiritual communities and centres – including Gaia House, an intensive meditation centre in Devon, and the Sharpham North Community near Totnes.

Christopher is a member and supporter of a number of organizations working for people and planet. He is on the international board of the Buddhist Peace Fellowship. He has stood for parliament as the Green Party candidate in the constituency where he lives. More than 1000 of his tapes on spirituality are available. Christopher lives in Totnes with his young daughter, Nshorna.

SPIRIT FOR CHANGE

Voices of Hope
for a World in Crisis

CHRISTOPHER TITMUSS

GREEN
PRINT

First published in 1989 by
Green Print
an imprint of The Merlin Press Ltd
10 Malden Road, London NW5 3HR

ISBN 1 85425 015 9

1 2 3 4 5 6 7 8 9 10 :: 99 98 97 96 95 94 93 92 91 90 89

Typeset by Input Typesetting Ltd in 9½/11pt Sabon

Printed in England by Biddles Ltd., Guildford
on recycled paper

*Earth which has seemed too large
must now be seen in its smallness.
We live in a closed system,
absolutely dependent on earth
and on each other for our lives
and for those of succeeding generations.
The many things that divide us
are therefore of infinitely less importance
than the interdependence and danger
that unite us.*

From the message to 'our 3.5 billion neighbours on planet earth,'
by biologists from six countries meeting in Menton, France, May,
1970.

Acknowledgements

Between 1984 and 1989, I travelled in England, Continental Europe, India, Thailand, Sri Lanka, Australia and the United States where I conducted thirty taped interviews and collected material for this book. This is a selection of those interviews. To all the people I interviewed who kindly found time in their full schedules to meet with me, I express heartfelt thanks. Each one communicated a spiritual awareness and understanding of the issues affecting people and the planet.

I also wish to express my appreciation to Henrietta Rogell who has worked continuously with me on the typescript. Her help with the editing and with the many details in the preparation of the typescript have been invaluable.

Many thanks to various friends who set up several of the interviews for me including David Arnott, James Baraz, Christine Engels, Catherine Ingram and Satish Kumar. Without their co-operation, this book would not have been possible.

Heartfelt thanks also goes to Gwanwyn Williams, who kindly gave much assistance in transcribing many of the tapes.

Also special thanks to Evelyn Sweeney, Rose Deiss, Maurice Ash and Walter Schwarz.

To all these people and many more, I express gratitude for their support and encouragement in this endeavour.

May all people, creatures and the planet
live in peace and harmony.

Contents

SOCIAL ACTION

PSYCHOLOGY OF CHANGE

A Personal Preface

It is dawn on a winter's morning in Totnes, a small town in Devon, England. The frost has registered itself in the night. As I look out of my window, I can see the cars parked in the suburban street, their windows and paintwork coated in the frost. I sit here wondering how the day will unfold for the residents of one little street of fifty eight homes in this corner of the countryside. Is it possible for global awareness to find expression in our daily activities?

As I look out from my terraced house over the rooftops of the houses opposite, I can see the green and brown fields and the occasional tree standing in its solitude. Here we live in our suburban streets; over there, within the gaze of our eyes, stands the earth and the rivers that sustain our lives and our organism.

A man emerges from his front door. He hurries across his garden to the waiting car. He's just moved round to open the car boot. He has an aerosol can in his hand with which to spray the car windows to remove the icy chill. The car key turns in the ignition, the engine turns over and over in an endeavour to warm up. Out of the exhaust gush clouds of smoke as the carbon monoxide fumes enter into the atmosphere. The car moves up the road. Later in the morning, I shall take my daughter, Nshorna, to school by car.

I have knocked on numerous doors in various parts of this area, particularly for the Green Party, and have had the opportunity to listen to a diversity of views and opinions of those willing to share their concerns with a stranger on the doorstep. After such communication with people, whether at their home or in the high street, I am left with a variety of impressions. I like to think that these impressions are reasonably accurate, reflecting the attitudes and thoughts of a cross-section of the general public.

One thing I have learnt is that television plays a great role in determining the response of the householder. The average person in Britain watches more than twenty one hours a week of television, nearly a day a week given to staring at the box. No other instrument in our consumer society has so effectively captured the attention of the people. All differences – social, political, age, class, religious – dissolve when attention is glued to the hypnotic screen.

And what does it tell us? Among other things:

- More than 40,000 of the world's children die every day from malnutrition.

- We spend more than £1 million per minute on the arms race.

- Europe spends more than £1 million per day to store its food mountains.

- One in six of the world's population live in absolute poverty.

- In any given fortnight some 50% of the people in the West are taking medicine.

- One in three men in Britain will have a heart attack before the age of 60.

- More than 4,000,000 animals die every year from experiments in Britain's laboratories.

- 70% of the available water in India is polluted by chemicals and sewage.

- More than 50% of West Germany's forests are dying from acid rain.

- The USA consumes more than 750 million trees per year.

- Thousands of Swedish lakes are dying from acid rain.

- More than 30,000 people, a good size town, die from lung cancer alone every year in Britain.

- Countless numbers are threatened, tortured, imprisoned and murdered for working for social justice.

- More Americans have died from AIDS than were killed in the Vietnam War.

- One species becomes extinct every half an hour.

- A tropical rainforest, equivalent to the size of England and Wales, is being destroyed every year.

- The first hole, the size of the U.S.A., has appeared in the ozone layer which protects people and the earth from the sun's ultraviolet rays.

- The increase in carbon dioxide contributes to the greenhouse effect threatening dramatic changes in climate and weather patterns.

And so on and so on.

Early morning, midday and evening television communicates the news that provides instant and sometimes shocking facts. It pinpoints what is happening to our world, to ourselves, to our environment. But although we have become so well-informed, we have also become such passive creatures. We withdraw into the armchair, with the television as our consort, like a recluse who locks himself or herself away for the rest of their life.

Nonetheless, people *do* have views on virtually every major issue of our time – nuclear weapons, unemployment, AIDS, famine, human rights, tropical rainforests, natural resources, cancer, animal rights and so on. If there has been a programme on the television recently on that particular theme, the person is likely to be much more animated while expressing their view. People *are* concerned. They do experience an awareness of reality beyond their personal lives as well as issues which directly affect them.

But, although people are genuinely concerned and reasonably knowledgeable about issues facing them and the planet, their comments are often qualified with such one-liners as:

'What can you do?'

'You can't stop progress.'

'You've got to look after yourself in this world.'

'Everything will work out for the best.'

'The world has got to come to an end sometime, hasn't it?'

'Crisis? What crisis?'

'It's too late.'

'I don't have time.'

'It's hard enough trying to make ends meet.'

'I'm too old.'

'I support what you're doing but . . .'

'It's God's will.'

However, there are a considerable number of people who, in spite of such reservations as these, are interested to find ways and means to *express* their concern for people and the planet. I would describe them as closet activists. They may or may not go to work, they may or may not watch television, but to some degree they have retained a commitment to a way of life free from greed, competitiveness and the sole pursuit of pleasure and profit. Such people may be exploring spirituality, therapy and healing. Or they may be working for others, for animals or the environment.

No doubt some of us can remember a turning point in which a sense of the inter-connectedness between ourselves and the planet was reawakened. For me, this fusion of personal and global awareness took place on a flight to Boston, USA, in the summer of 1980.

I was sitting in a window seat aimlessly staring out of the window into the summer's day sky and the ocean below. Without preparation or thought, two mental wires suddenly fused together. One wire was the spiritual element in which I had a sustained and abiding interest. The other was the political field which had laid dormant for a decade. What struck me on this otherwise forgettable flight was that spiritual awareness, self-knowledge, meditation, psychotherapy, religious beliefs and experiences are potentially the raw material for an active political awareness expressing reverence for life, which truly embraces all people, animals and nature.

The next step was to inform myself not only about the state of the planet but also to explore the various perceptions and insights of the social-political analysts, historians and activists: Marx, Gandhi, Schumacher, Mumford, Fromm, Lewis, Martin Luther King, and books by concerned contemporary women, such as Susan Griffin and Jean Baker Miller. I came to regard the 'Manifesto for a Sustainable Society' by Britain's Green Party as a remarkable blueprint for a society to change its harmful political and economic system for a caring relationship for people and planet.

I committed myself for the next three years to reading one book per month. I took out subscriptions to various informative magazines and became a member of about 15 organizations that serve global interests. I attended conferences, public talks and meetings, and step by step, my awareness and knowledge deepened. In small ways I began to express my concerns through participation in some of the issues of our time.

In recent years, there has been an increasing loss of faith in and rejection of violent left-wing revolutions. There has begun to emerge a coherent philosophy with fresh insights embracing a far-reaching global view based on the inter-connectedness of all levels of life. This quietly mobilizing revolution is characterized by being non-violent and green.

One of the various features of the non-violent movements towards social and global change is the noticeable lack of leaders. The days when the masses followed Moses out of the land of bondage are for the most part finished. Today we are moving away, thankfully, from the charismatic and visionary individual, to small collectives specializing in particular fields for the health, welfare and liberation of the planet from its pain.

Who can name a leader of the peace movement, despite the fact that in the 1980s millions have taken to the streets to protest about the massive arms industry? Who can name a leader of the women's movement despite the fact that millions of women are untying the social knots that have imprisoned them? Who can name a leader of the green movement, despite the fact that membership of green organizations grows dramatically by the year? Who can name a leader of the spiritual-psychotherapy movement, despite the wide-spread involvement in the philosophies of the East, meditation, liberation theology, the yogas and inner change of mind states and consciousness?

The people interviewed in this book are not to be interpreted as the high priests or priestesses of their particular fields. They are not people we need to project our hopes on to. Rather they are voices of concern. For the most part, they are articulate voices whose activities communicate what might be described as a global psychology. I have spoken to them about their commitments. Eight of them have participated in a number of retreats on engaged spirituality with me.

Hopefully, others of us among the now estimated four billion will join this movement to safeguard and liberate the planet, a movement which has no fixed name, no special ideology, no charismatic leadership. Certainly the people who were interviewed would not all be in agreement with each other. And an hour-long interview is going to reveal very little about their spectrum of views. What I can say is that each one communicates to me some awakening of heart and mind to immediate reality.

The spiritual is a constant thread throughout this book. Spirituality, however we may define it, is not something we need to divorce from the rest of our life. For myself, spirituality embraces both the transcendent and the immanent. As the transcendent, I experience a profoundly liberating sense of mystery. As the immanent, I experience a deep reverence towards life expressed through action. There are people who would never think of themselves as 'spiritual' yet their awareness, thoughts and actions reveal an ongoing respect and reverence for life. Equally, there are people who think of themselves as 'spiritual' but cannot see further than the end of their noses. No doubt, we all live with blind spots.

It is essential to recognize that the future of not only the human race but all species and all the countless expressions of life depends upon our capacity and heartfelt willingness to look at life as a totality rather than through the coloured glasses of 'me' and 'mine'.

Recently I received a postcard with the following passage printed on it. 'They' can be translated as any one of the global problems that affect all of us now or affects the quality of life of our children and our children's children.

> *First they came for the Jews*
> *and I did not speak out—*
> *because I was not a Jew.*
>
> *Then they came for the communists*
> *and I did not speak out—*
> *because I was not a communist.*
>
> *Then they came for the trade unionists*
> *and I did not speak out—*
> *because I was not a trade unionist*
>
> *Then they came for me—*
> *and there was no one left*
> *to speak out for me.*

> Pastor Niemoeller
> (victim of the Nazis)

Finally, I would like this book and other similar books of this decade to be read by future generations – if there will be any – so they too will know that in this long enduring time of serious human and global problems there were voices of concern, there was a spirit for change.

Peace,

Christopher Titmuss
Totnes, Devon, England
Winter, 1989

INNER AWARENESS

Reduction of needs

*An interview with Satish Kumar
Devon, England*

During the 1960s, Satish Kumar and a companion made a two and a half year walk for peace from his home country of India through Pakistan, Afghanistan, Iran, the Soviet Union, Poland, East and West Germany, Belgium, France, England, and America. They carried no money on this 8000 mile walk, depending totally on the hospitality and goodwill of the people of each country. The story of this marathon walk is told in his book, *No Destination*. Satish was offered an award from the Soviet Union for the book, but he declined it, saying that Russia must first release dissident writers who are imprisoned.

Satish entered into the religious life as a 9-year-old boy when he became a monk in the Jain religion. This is a religion in India famous for its respect and total dedication to uphold and protect all sentient life from pain. By the time he was 18 years old, he had decided to combine spiritual practices with social action; he left the monkhood and joined the Gandhian movement under Vinoba Bhave.

Satish joined Vinoba in persuading landlords to donate land to the landless—the aim of which was to establish a peaceful economic revolution. After some time, Vinoba encouraged Satish and his friend to make the long walk for peace.

In 1968 Satish was invited to England by Christian Aid to establish and direct the London School of Non-Violence. He taught courses in non-violent action, sustainable economics and development in the Third World. During this period he became a close friend of Dr E. F. Schumacher, a founding father of the Green

Movement and author of the classic of Green economics, *Small Is Beautiful*.

Satish is one of the major inspirations in the international Green movement. Throughout the years he has initiated various projects as a vehicle to implement, in practical ways, his concerns for people and planet.

In the early 1970s, Satish was invited to become editor of *Resurgence*, a thoughtful and influential journal of green economics, green politics, ecology and holistic awareness. His enthusiasm for green issues is reflected in the positive outlook of *Resurgence*, a magazine in the forefront of ecological consciousness. After the death of E. F. Schumacher in 1977, he founded the Schumacher Society in honour of the economist. He has been president of the society since its foundation and has organized and presided over the internationally respected Schumacher Memorial Lectures held in Britain every autumn.

Satish believes that it is the responsibility of the state to fund education and that the responsibility for curriculum and management rests with the school governors, teachers, parents and children. So in 1982, Satish founded the Small School in Hartland, North Devon with nine children to follow through with his ideology. The enrolment has now increased to more than thirty children. Other areas in the country appreciate what has been created and are now considering starting Small Schools for their children.

The latest project that Satish has instigated is the establishment of a new publishing house, called Green Books, specializing in green and global issues.

Satish lives in Hartland with his wife and two children, a cow and a vegetable allotment. Although living in a somewhat isolated region of Devon, the family does not own a car. Visitors come frequently from around the world to his home.

The interview with Satish was conducted at the Sharpham Community, where he had been giving one of his numerous public talks. Satish explores some of his life's influences, of which his mother was one. It is not the first time that he has spoken of her with such love and devotion.

SK: I was born into a very orthodox Jain family. My mother was a very, very devout Jain and what I learnt about the Jain religion was mainly from her. The most important thing I realized, which is even more clear now, was that my mother saw everything in the world, whether a plant, a tree, a bird, a piece of grass, a rock or human being, as having a spirit. And therefore she practised a complete and utter non-violence to all beings, living and not living.

CT: Her perception that everything has spirit or soul brought forth a great reverence for life.

SK: Reverence. That's the word. She thought that as human beings we have to practise reduction of our needs, a reduction of dependence on other things and other beings. Therefore, for example, we practised complete vegetarianism. A Jain on no account will kill an animal to eat. That is a reduction of need. My mother made a list of fifty items, including rice, mangoes, cauliflower, lentils and certain spices and said, 'Among all the vegetarian foods, I will eat only these 50 items.' So her needs were reduced. When it came to travel she would not go in any direction that she wanted. She would say, 'I will only travel twenty miles today, only in the eastern direction, going and coming back.' She would not go off somewhere on the spur of the moment wherever she liked because even when you are travelling you are taking space, you are using the earth, you are treading on the grass and harming beings living or not living. Therefore she would reduce her travel needs. With clothing she would say, 'I need only twenty items of clothing.' At no time would she have more than twenty items. The moment she buys one new item of clothing she would have to make sure that one piece of clothing is old enough to give away or to use as rags. So we can reduce our needs by observing how many possessions we have. The most fundamental principles of Jain religion are non-possession and non-violence.

CT: You had this influence right from conception. In your own way you took it a step further by becoming a monk.

SK: That's right. When I was 9 years old I came in close contact with the monks because my mother was always going to meet with them. The monks said, 'If you are living in the world with a family, a business, a house, however much care you take, you can never practise non-violence and non-possession to its utmost limits. Only by becoming a monk and renouncing all possessions and all forms of violence, as well as renouncing family and home, can you really set an example of complete and total non-violence and non-possession.' And that idea attracted me very much. I thought at least some people are practising an extreme form of non-violence and non-attachment; not a middle path but an extreme path. It would be a good thing to show the world how little one really needs. That really attracted me very much even though I was only nine. And that is where I believe that something must have come to me from my previous life, that at the age of nine I could have such a determined and passionate thought to become a monk in such an extreme form.

CT: You made a very long journey by foot from India to the West. What was the impact of the West upon you?

SK: In the beginning when I first came to the West it was a cultural shock for me. When I saw people were acquiring things they didn't really need I was shocked. At heart, I was a monk, though at this time I had left the outer form of the monastic life. I felt this kind of acquisitive and materialistic culture of the West was having an influence and impact on the whole world. And perhaps it was useful for me to talk to and live with people in the West while practising some of the principles of non-possession and non-violence, such as being vegetarian, not having the usual possessions of life, like a television or car which people take for granted as a normal part of living. They always ask me, how can you live in the countryside in such a remote place like Hartland in North Devon and not have a car? How do you manage? How do you move about? And I say that I walk wherever I need to walk. I have two legs. People have forgotten that they have two legs and these legs can take you anywhere.

CT: How did you become exposed to Fritz Schumacher's teachings and the Green philosophy?

SK: When I came to live in the West, because of the cultural shock, I started to look around for kindred spirits. I looked for people who had some spiritual, ecological, green values which were in keeping with my Jain training and background. During that time I came across an article by E. F. Schumacher called 'Buddhist Economics'. Schumacher could have called this 'Jain Economics'. In essence, Jain economics and Buddhist economics are very similar. Immediately being gripped and enchanted by what I read, I wrote to Schumacher. I was very happy to receive his response and we set up a meeting.

Immediately we got on very well together. From the first meeting in 1968 we became such good friends that we thought we had known each other for a long time even though we had not met before. From then until the time that he died in 1977 we remained very close. Schumacher was closely associated with *Resurgence* magazine and it was through him and the former editor, John Papworth, that I came to be editor. They said I was a Gandhian and a Jain and Schumacher said, 'The Jain religion must be one of the most ecological religions in the world. Therefore if you bring those values and combine them with the conservation and the ecological movement of the West, that will be a very useful thing to do.'

CT: You had years of contact with Schumacher, who is regarded as a founding father of the green movement. How would you describe his major themes?

SK: You can find the key to Schumacher's thinking in three sentences. Number one is – keep it small. Number two is – keep it simple. Number three is – keep it non-violent. Whether it is a technology, a social or political organization, or economics that you're dealing with, you keep it small on a human scale so that the intimacy of human relationship is never destroyed. Bigness always undermines the human scale and human relationship. The moment you grow too big you have to follow a certain set of rules to work things out.

CT: Then those of us in the Green movement are in a paradox. Schumacher and others say, 'Keep it small,' and we are also saying we want the green movement to grow.

SK: If you keep it small, simple and non-violent, there is still room for growth, but in quality not just in quantity. Our scientific and technological work is always looking for quantitative growth which can be measured. Schumacher says that you can grow inwardly; you can improve the quality in your relationship, in your homes, villages, farms and factories, and thus find a happier environment with a more wholesome lifestyle. And that's the growth which he talked about. He didn't talk about growing in numbers. He was talking about growing in the quality of life.

CT: You have lived a life of simplicity, severity and austerity in India. Now you live in the West and all that goes with that. Have you wondered whether there has been some compromise of values?

SK: I don't think there has been a compromise. I think that by going through the rigorous discipline of a Jain monk I have learnt to be inwardly detached. Once you have learnt that stage of being then you can be in the midst of the hubbly bubbly of the world and still be detached. I have learnt that way and I feel quite detached and not overwhelmed by the possessions nor in any way oppressed by the Western world.

CT: In this detached attitude toward possessions, is it your view that possessions only have a utilitarian value?

SK: I would say, possessions not only have a utilitarian value; possessions are transformed as objects of relationship and therefore, even those objects become your companions and friends. Like this jumper I'm wearing. It is not a utilitarian jumper but is a jumper with which I have a friendship and a relationship. The jumper is protecting me and I am protecting the jumper. I am looking after the jumper, washing it, cleaning it and keeping it neat and tidy so that in ten years' time I might be wearing the same jumper. I am looking after it as a friend. In return the jumper is being very compassionate and very kind to me. It is protecting me from the rain, from the cold and so on. So the possessions I have are few. I have them not as utilitarian objects but as friends.

In the same way if I am in a home, it is God's home; it is a sacred home, a holy place. It is the home where I can sit down. I can meditate. I can have guests. I can offer hospitality. I can look after my children. I can let them grow there. I can love my family. So a home is a spiritual place and not a matter of status, or of possession or investment. I don't possess such thoughts at all. I have no interest in its monetary value. My interest is in its spiritual value. If we can transform our attitude in that way, then everything that we use to make our home, all the materials of the earth – slates, stones, wood, fibre, etc. – contribute to making home life rich, spiritual and sacred.

CT: You had the value of a mother deeply committed to ecological values. You had the discipline and training of the Jain monkhood. Most of us have neither and therefore, our models have been different.

SK: People who are concerned with such matters as you expressed have to find kindred spirits. One, two, ten, no matter how many, because kindred spirits can give mutual support and mutual nourishment to each other. In the Jain and Buddhist tradition this is called 'sangha' – people giving nourishment to each other. So I would say that people who are seeking something different, which is spiritual, sacred, fundamental and in harmony with themselves, their work and nature, have to seek out people who are supportive to that approach and not live surrounded by people who are always encouraging them to buy more, possess more, go faster, become successful, gain richness and fame. If you haven't got the discipline of a Jain or Buddhist, or a background like I had with my mother, at least now you can find kindred spirits. They are certainly around. Perhaps you can find companionship in your neighbourhood, so you are supported and so you are not living in the desert of materialism.

CT: Would you say that in the last fifteen years the desert of materialism has been more deeply questioned?

SK: Yes, I see that. When I came fifteen years ago to Britain, if you went around looking for a vegetarian restaurant, you would have to search hard to find five or ten in the whole country. Now in almost every town you can find one. You can say the same thing about wholefood. When I came, food was mass-produced and mostly tinned. People wanted fast food and junk food. They were just not interested in wholesome food. What they ate was not really their concern. It was much more a matter of convenience. Now people are concerned with what they eat, the kind of food and how it is grown. So wholefood shops have sprung up.

Fifteen years ago the word 'meditation' was a weird word. Now we can learn to meditate and be part of a normal society. So the consciousness has changed. These are examples that show that something is going on. Something is happening. Even though the governments and financial institutions, the multi-national corporations, the schools and hospitals have not changed, the individual people within them are questioning.

CT: These questions are being asked, yet there seems to be very little inroad in terms of Buddhist economics. The emphasis of the present Western governments, which influences the teachers of economics in our schools, is to stress a wealth-creating society.

SK: I agree with you. Government thinking and policy has not changed, but on the grass roots level I think there are many more Buddhist economics-oriented projects and businesses now than there were fifteen years ago. In the last census in Britain the population of the big cities is decreasing and the rural areas increasing. Devon has increased by six per cent and Norfolk and Suffolk by nine per cent. The population of the larger cities of Birmingham, Manchester, London, and Glasgow is decreasing. The trend has changed and the trend is towards going back to the countryside, starting a small business, a craft shop or a wholefood shop, entering into a livelihood which is more in harmony with yourself and your ideals. And those things are growing. It is my hope that in the next five or ten years unemployed people will find some self-employment which is useful, ecologically sound and spiritually rewarding. I think the problem is not unemployment. The problem is employment. People must have the chance to find good work.

CT: You are speaking about the form of employment?

SK: People are working in nuclear power stations; people are working in factories where they are mass-producing cars, armaments, clothing, televisions and newspapers. All these kinds of jobs are essentially soul–destroying, spirit–destroying, nature–destroying, world–destroying, and planet–destroying. The thing is that all civilizations come, rise and fall. The Roman empire, the Egyptian empire, the British empire, all have come and gone. Now we are going through the industrial empire, where technology, science, rationalism and analytical thinking are dominant. As a result, our arts, our work, our mode of production, our culture has been affected by industrial, mechanistic growth. This will come to an end, as every civilization has to come to an end, since the world is impermanent and changing and nothing can last for ever. We are not going back but we are transforming the present structure to be much more human.

People call 'transformation' going back. Going back to what? Going back to the first principle of love and compassion in mutual help and support. And these values can create more harmonious modes of work and production and more creativity in the arts. We have to talk in terms of transformation rather than returning to a primitive or pre-industrial society.

CT: You and your family have spent recent years in a remote North Devon village. What have you been doing there?

SK: I have been living. [He smiles.] I think that I can do nothing more important than to live, to be. But outwardly people see how

I live, namely I edit the magazine *Resurgence* because I think it is very important that we don't live with our ideas in isolation. We are not isolated beings; we are part of this network of society. Communicating with society is one of the major concerns that I have. Through *Resurgence* I have been able to offer a forum and a platform, a medium of communication, so that people can see a different way of living, of thinking, of working. So *Resurgence* has been my main work, but I don't do it as a job or profession; I do it as a service to society, a communication with society. I see it in context with the rest of my living: with my family, working on the land, growing food, looking after the cow and being a little bit self-sufficient. This context is very important to me. If you see my life, one third is devoted to my intellectual work on *Resurgence*. The second third is devoted to my physical activities, like working on the garden, milking the cow, cooking the food, cleaning the house. The remaining third is devoted to the emotional sphere, my relationship with my children, wife and friends, with my guests, when receiving people or staying with others. Throughout these three spheres there is a thread which you cannot see. You can see the beads but you cannot see the thread. The thread is the spiritual. So my intellectual work, my physical work and my emotional work are in the service of the spirit.

CT: What does the word 'spiritual' mean for you?

SK: To me 'spiritual' means something which is more than meets the eye. For example, I talked about my jumper and my relationship with it. That relationship is something that you cannot see outwardly. It is my inner spiritual understanding and awareness, and this I am trying to develop all the time through meditation, study, and through communication. It also involves the question of service. It touches upon my relationship with my wife, June, with my children and neighbours and with people who are in need. Now what is the inspiration for that service? What is the inspiration for working in the garden? The inspiration is spiritual. So all of my activities have to stem from that basis.

This spiritual approach to life, which is so subtle, which cannot be described in words or analysed or really even be spoken about but can be felt, is where you can find a sense of fulfilment. The meaning of life can only be fulfilled through this spiritual awareness. For a human being who does not feel fulfilled, the first thing is to stop wherever you are. If you are not happy with your life, your work, with the way you are and you don't really know where you are going and you feel lost, you stop. There is no point in continuing to go. Then you will meet some passers by. When you do, ask them the way. Somebody will help. There will be those who will say, 'I don't know,' and those who'll say, 'Don't bother me.' After asking with real inquiry, somebody you meet will know where you want to go. And yet, you have to find your own way, not follow where somebody else is going or go where somebody else wants you to go. We all have our destiny and our path. But there are people who will help you to find your way and they are the people I call kindred spirits.

CT: We may say that the path itself, when deeply comprehended, is so fulfilling that there is no destination.

SK: Yes. Yes. There is no destination. Life is here and all the time we are moving without a destination.

'Don't close off to pain'

An interview with Dr Joanna Macy
Devon, England

Dr Joanna Macy, a Buddhist scholar and teacher, is primarily interested in applying the principles of Buddhism to situations that we face in life on a day-to-day basis. Not surprisingly, then, one of the main themes apparent in Joanna's work is the theme of interdependence. This theme emphasizes a unity and support among the people on our planet rather than the isolation and powerlessness so predominant in our societies today. Joanna has said the root problem for dealing with issues is this sense of powerlessness. She is committed to bringing about a fundamental change in the psyche of people so that we experience a sense of power and can express that power in a caring and loving way.

Several years ago, Joanna realized that as a human being, woman and mother, she was experiencing deep feelings with regard to the present planetary crisis. Through her communications with other women and men she perceived that these feelings were quite normal rather than the experience of only a handful of particularly sensitive people.

Drawing on her wealth of experience in meditation, psychotherapy and general systems theory, Joanna began facilitating workshops called 'Despair and Empowerment' for people concerned about the state of the planet. Her workshops helped people work with their feelings of despair and powerlessness. In 1979, out of this work and her public talks on the psychological realities of the nuclear age, Joanna founded Interhelp, an international network of people concerned not only with peace and social justice but also with transforming any perceptions that inhibit their capacity to respond effectively to global realities.

In her book *Despair and Personal Power in the Nuclear Age* Joanna writes, 'Despair and Empowerment work helps us to increase our awareness of these developments (threat of nuclear war, the progressive destruction of our life-support system, and the unprecedented spread of human misery) without feeling over-whelmed by the dread, grief, anger and sense of powerlessness that they arouse in us. These feelings are largely suppressed and this repression tends to paralyse us. We need to help each other to process this information on an effective level.'

Her book not only touches on planetary perils and quotes numer-ous psychological responses but also describes a number of exercises that enable individuals and groups to look full face at what is happening to our world and to ourselves in the process.

Her workshops also include a number of exercises that aid in releasing a whole variety of emotions including fear, joy, anger, rage, love, hurt and gratitude. Through the process of allowing the range of feelings and shared experiences to flow, another level of contact and communication with the whole of life is revealed. What comes out of these workshops is a clear release of fresh energies and a sense, to varying depths, of solidarity with people and planet.

In the late seventies Joanna became interested in a project in Sri Lanka called the Sarvodaya movement. She wanted to know more about these people living in the villages and applying Buddhist principles to all areas of their life, including health, education, agriculture and the arts. In 1980, with the help of a grant from the Ford Foundation, Joanna went to Sri Lanka to live with them for a year. She wrote a book called *Dharma and Development*, which describes her experiences in Sri Lanka and their influence on her, as well as the nature and purpose of the Sarvodaya movement.

Joanna at present lives with her husband, Francis, in Berkeley, California and they have three grown children, Peggy, Jack and Chris. In October 1986, she flew to England to lead a Despair and Empowerment workshop and to speak at the annual Schumacher Society lecture in Bristol. She stayed at my home in Totnes and there we taped the following interview.

CT: There has been a general conception that men are superior to women, human beings are superior to creatures, creatures are superior to trees and plants, plants are superior to rocks. This hierarchy has been created in the minds of people. How can we look at this world in a fresh way?

JM: We can start with our bodies. We are made of the dance of organic molecules produced through an action that goes back so far that we can say we are starstuff evolving. This is a wonder, a miracle. I look at my hand and I see four and a half billion years of life on this particular planet. I look at that with awe. I behold you, Christopher, that you are a product of this particular planet in a medium-size solar system off to the edge of this galaxy. Innumerable adventures have moulded what you are, what I am.

CT: The body is a remarkable composition. Sometimes that observation arises spontaneously. Is it useful to explore and reflect on the interdependence of the body and world?

JM: Yes. We need to be aware of that. We also need to be aware of the fact that we are appearing in this post-industrial culture after a millennium of conditioned thought where matter is viewed as less worthy than mind, where it is viewed even with some contempt or disgust. A dichotomy has been posited between mind and matter and one set above the other.

CT: Do you mean that we have reduced matter to the whims of the mind?

JM: In our culture, conditioned by Newton, Descartes and the so-called Western Enlightenment, the relationship between mind and matter has always been a puzzle for us. You have those who say that only the mind is real and matter is not. On the other hand, you have those who say only that which you can touch, weigh and measure is ultimately real. The Jungian psychologist and thinker, James Hillman, points out that materialism is often a product of the mind's fear of matter. Matter, mater, mother. A paradoxical dynamic gets set up when you polarize mind and matter. When you do, then the goal of the spiritual path, whether it's to be enlightened or saved, becomes the extraction of mind from the toils of matter. You see that in a number of religious traditions. And when you try to escape from that which you are dependent upon, a love–hate relationship gets set up between the ego, mind and matter. Matter or the natural world is seen as a trap. You may try to be very austere or ascetic in order to extract yourself from matter, or else this love–hate relationship leads to a materialistic drive to dominate and acquire.

CT: A materialist or hedonist might say, 'It's not a trap. I like matter. I like things. I want more. Why shouldn't I get more?'

JM: Four-legged creatures, for the most part, don't eat more than their bodies can assimilate. They don't get sick from overeating. It is the mind's greed that makes us want to acquire more than we can use. Materialism is the greed to acquire. It is really a mental phenomenon. Money is a beautiful example of this. You can't eat that piece of money, or wear it, or make love to it. You can't sing songs to it or hear it or walk in it or smell it. It's an abstraction, an example of a kind of psychosis. When the Buddha talked about greed or grasping he mentioned four objects. The other three that he mentioned were all mental: grasping after ego, grasping after views and being right, and grasping after rituals.

CT: A person may say, 'I am aware of this grasping but the awareness does not seem to stop it or even brake the force of it.'

JM: We are taught that we have a lot of needs. Our culture, conditioning and advertising tells us how we need to look or smell. Ivan Illich, the writer on contemporary society, talks about the creation of needs for our capitalist system. It is very easy to fall into the illusion that our needs are many. Here mindfulness can be an extremely important and powerful friend. As Gandhi said, 'The world has enough for everyone's need but not for everyone's greed.' We can then begin to experience the freedom that is here for us when we liberate ourselves from socially-induced needs.

CT: So one important aspect is mindfulness and awareness of our mental condition. Elevating ourselves over nature is assumed to be the true reality. How can we individually and collectively contribute to dissolving this division?

JM: Consciousness is co-arising with physical and mental experience. There isn't a consciousness all by itself in a pure, rarified, absolute state. Consciousness always has an occasion for its presence. We are therefore continually in dialogue with our environment. We can never be a disembodied monad; we are products of interaction. We only want to be free when we feel trapped by nature. Life is a dance that we can enjoy and it is quite wondrous. We exist in interplay, in interaction. Our senses tell us that. Each sense gate or faculty of seeing, hearing, smelling, tasting and touching tells us that we are engaged in interaction.

CT: In your work and travels you meet women and men who are looking at the global situation and experiencing a great deal of personal pain as a result of what they see. Would you say they are perceiving this in the world or is the world mirroring a state of mind?

JM: I think it is being perceived in the world. And I'd like to say that I have yet to meet anyone who is not in grief over what they see happening. Anyone who is conscious today sees that there is hunger, that there is inequality and progressive destruction. Anyone who is to any degree awake to the conditions of the world knows we cannot count on there being a future.

CT: That includes the people you have met in the East.

JM: Many in the East and in the Third World have immediate survival issues uppermost in their mind – feeding the family, getting shelter. Among affluent Westerners this suffering appears as awareness of a kind of global pain. It does not necessarily depend on one's politics. It is even felt among those who say they aren't interested in reducing armaments or the decimation of the rainforests. Everywhere there is a dis-ease, a malaise, a grief that we cannot count on there being a future. I think for most people this pain for the world is barely conscious; it is seldom discussed. There is resistance to painful transformation. So when painful information is offered about the effects of Chernobyl or another nuclear accident, or the spreading of the deserts or the poisoning of the seas, for example, people block that out. That's a self-protection mechanism, to protect the mind from fear, especially the fear that the mind will lose control. 'I can't bear to think about it because I might fall apart. I can't bear to think about this because I might get stuck in despair. I might shatter into a thousand pieces. Don't ask me to take it in.' There is fear of experiencing the pain that goes with this information.

CT: So how do you respond to someone who comes up and says, 'I can't take it anymore. I can't take this pain that I see all around me?'

JM: I invite them to breathe. In my workshops I use a breathing method which is 2000 years old. It comes out of the early Tibetan tradition and was originally used to help people develop compassion. That's really what we are talking about. We are talking about suffering *with* our world. And to suffer with our world is literally what compassion means.

CT: Are you saying, 'Don't close off to the pain.'

JM: Yes. To close off to the pain is to go dead inside. It is a form of death. I believe the greatest danger we face is our denial – thinking that we can't look at the dangers – in economics, in the environment or with the military. We imagine we are so fragile, that if we look at what's happening we'll break.

CT: But it takes courage to open up the heart and mind to the pain of the planet. Where is this courage going to come from?

JM: I think it is quite easy. That's why I prefer to work in groups. We need each other in this. This is a very natural process for us. We are made to be open and interactive with each other. Just look at my hands or my eyes or ears. As human life evolved on the planet we became more vulnerable to the world. We evolved sensitive protuberances. What we are made for is to connect. Just as the cells and the neurons in our bodies are made to connect with each other and spin complex systems, so are we. This, I believe, is the teaching in the *dharma* [the teachings of the Buddha]. We are made for interaction. By using the breath, for example, we can experience the taking in of information about the planet without breaking down.

CT: What is the breathing technique that you use in your workshops?

JM: Focusing on the breath you note the sensations that accompany it, whether at the nostrils, throat or lungs. You watch the breathing in a very alert way like a cat by the mouse-hole. You begin to notice that you're not breathing by a choice of will but that you're being breathed by life. Then you picture the breath as a stream of air coming up through the nose, down through the throat, lungs, and then out again to link with the living, breathing web of life made up of all beings around you. When the images of suffering come to the surface of your mind, you allow that pain, like a dark substance, to be carried on the breath stream into your very being and through your heart. You don't hold on to it but let it flow back out into the healing resources of the web of life. You are simply allowing yourself to be present, letting the pain pass through your heart. That's all you are asking yourself to do.

CT: So there are three important reasons for compassionate breathing. One is to give ourselves greater capacity to deal with the suffering that we hear and see every day. The second would be to deal with the accumulated suffering and pain. The third is that the breathing helps reveal our organic intimacy with life, interdependent and co-existent.

JM: Yes. And, I would add another. During the Vietnam war, our president Lyndon Johnson, said, 'Don't bring me a problem unless you can bring me a solution.' We tend to feel that we cannot take in any grief or problem unless we have the answer to it. That's backwards. We have to expose ourselves to a situation, stand naked before it, so to speak, before an appropriate response to the problem can arise. Breathing in this way helps us, quite literally, to stop putting up an armour against bad news and to allow it to connect more intimately with us.

CT: When you give a public talk I would imagine that a number of listeners block out some of the things you say, as they would in other situations.

JM: Actually, I don't find much resistance. Once people allow themselves to engage in a practice, even a little bit, it becomes self-validating. Often, at a big gathering, people are invited to do a version of the four abodes: loving kindness, compassion, joy for others and equanimity. I could just stand up and talk about them but that would be quite dull. So I prefer instead to invite the people to turn and use the person nearby as a meditation object. I then talk them through an exercise so that each of these four abodes can be experienced as they behold this other person. This is a practice that people can take away with them. You can do it sitting on a bus or looking across to someone at the check-out line at the supermarket. This is a way to practise deep inter-connectedness.

CT: If, as you say, the greatest problem is the denial of global realities, then the opening of the heart and exploring other ways and means to do that would be of primary urgency.

JM: It is. It also directly addresses the sense of being overwhelmed. When one looks at what is happening to our air, our water, our people, our planet, one can feel overwhelmed. What can just one out of nearly five billion people do except shut down or try to divert oneself? I like to emphasize that compassion has two sides to it. There is the side of opening to our pain for the world, which is compassion. The flip side is joy in each other's joy, power in each other's power, synergy. We can train ourselves to look at other people – be they lovers, friends or strangers – as resources. They are people from whom we can draw intelligence, love, ingenuity, for we are in the web of life *with* them. We can't solve the situation alone. We solve it in synergy with them. This can be experienced as a form of grace.

CT: In opening the heart and working with the pain, there comes about a flow of energy towards healing the planet and oneself. One begins to participate in that flow. But what do you mean by 'grace?' Where does 'grace' come from?

JM: I just love thinking about grace. It's hard to talk about it with our limited language. In Japanese, there are similar terms, 'jariki' and 'toriki', which mean 'own power' and 'other power'. Grace is the realization that you are part of something larger and receiving from it. You are carried by this realization like a wave carries you when you are surfing. You don't need to dredge up out of your own meagre resources all the love, patience, courage and inspiration that you are going to need. It's there in abundance. One of the first times I had a sense of grace was when I was going off to Sri Lanka. Some friends of mine came to say goodbye to me. I was going there for a year and I knew that I would be lonely. I knew there would be situations I would face that I wouldn't have an answer to. Together we invented a little ritual which we called 'the web'. It evoked my own creatureliness as part of the web of life. My friends spoke out, rather poetically, about things in the web which they wanted me to be aware of. One would say, 'Joanna, I give you the gift of the diving trout who is unafraid of the dark. May you be ever fearless of the dark.' Another said, 'May I give you the gift of the song thrush, who lets its voice be heard. May you never be fearful of speaking out.' These gifts were with me throughout the year.

In the Christian tradition in which I grew up, grace has come, by and large, to be equated with God's action: the experience of God holding me in the palm of his hand, the everlasting arms buoying me up. But grace can come just as well through other people. In the practice of the four abodes people can open to resources that come through others and are beyond what they think about themselves. For example, when I see your courage for what you have chosen to do with your life I could say, 'Oh my, Christopher has more courage than I.' It would make me feel rather cowardly which is a great foolishness. Or I could look with the mind of grace. The courage you show is in the web of life which called me into being. And I rejoice in that.

CT: So what emerges from the heart is appreciation free from comparisons.

JM: And free from envy. Grace is the power of life abounding around me that I can open myself to and channel. You don't have to stop and ask, 'Was that *my* idea or *your* idea? Was that *your* courage or *mine*?' These views become irrelevant. It's courage *happening*. It's ideas *happening*. It's love *flowing*. Because it happens in the interaction, it doesn't belong to anybody anyway.

CT: In the dynamic of this connectedness and interdependence we keep making contact with those giving support to life.

JM: Precisely. I would say that is one definition of grace – giving support to life. People can look at each other with great sensitivity to the other's pain but also with exaltation. They can look at each other and laugh and be happy knowing that there is a circulation of vitality that brings courage. You begin to dare to do things.

CT: With the sense of others there is a wider view.

JM: That's grace.

Watch the desires

An interview with U Nu
Bodh Gaya, India

U Nu made it perfectly clear before the interview began that he would not enter into any dialogue about the marriage of politics and Buddhism. He told me that if I brought up politics he would immediately stop the interview; he was willing to explore Buddhism as a spiritual practice but was no longer concerned with political activities and had no wish to go back to the time when he was the Prime Minister of Burma.

U Nu is a man with deep faith in Buddhism, the religion of his birth and of his country. His faith has carried him through numerous crises, both at the personal and social levels.

He was born in 1907 in the small township of Wakema in Burma. Even though he wanted to be an actor, he went to the capital, Rangoon, to study to be a schoolteacher. As a socialist he became politically active, joining the Thakin Party and founding the Red Dragon Book Society. It wasn't long before he drew the attention of the British Raj, and in 1940 he was imprisoned for his efforts to gain independence for Burma. When the Japanese invaded Burma, ostensibly to release Burma from British colonialism, U Nu was released and held a government post in the Ba Naw administration, basically a puppet government set up by the Japanese. During this time, however, U Nu was quietly campaigning to free Burma from the Japanese.

At the end of the war he was elected president of the Burmese Constituent Party and in July 1947 became Prime Minister of the now independent Burma. He was only forty years of age.

From the outset U Nu and the new cabinet attempted to bring about a synthesis of Buddhist principles, as contained in the Noble Eightfold Path, and a society grounded in socialist principles. The Noble Eightfold Path consists of Right Understanding, Right Attitude, Right Speech, Right Action, Right Livelihood, Right Effort, Right Awareness and Right Meditation.

It was this experiment, which lasted from 1947 to 1962, that came to the notice of E. F. Schumacher. In his famous chapter in *Small Is Beautiful* on 'Buddhist Economics' Schumacher begins by quoting a 1954 government report issued by U Nu: 'The new government sees no conflict between religious values and economic progress. Spiritual health and material well-being are not enemies, they are natural allies. We can blend successfully the religious and spiritual values of our heritage with the benefits of modern technology.'

Surviving a number of attempts to get him out of office, U Nu was eventually overthrown by a military coup in 1962. He was to spend yet another period in prison until 1966. Apart from a year's resignation from 1956 to 1957, he had been Prime Minister for fifteen years, a remarkable length of time, particularly in the sometimes fluctuating politics of a developing nation.

Since his release he has been very committed to the practice and propagation of the Theravada Buddhist tradition. He has studied and practised meditation extensively under the late Vipassana (insight) meditation teacher, Mahasi Sayadaw, who revitalized deep meditative practices among monks, nuns and lay people.

In 1980 U Nu founded the Burma Pitaka Association, whose aim is to promote English translations of the words of the Buddha. A number of important books in Pali, the language the Buddha spoke, were assigned to translators. In recent years U Nu has travelled to Europe to see for himself the way the Buddhist message is being established in the West.

From time to time, U Nu became a little annoyed with me for interrupting him. It was obvious that years ago he had been interviewed on countless occasions by reporters when he was Prime Minister. Perhaps he sensed (correctly) that I was a news reporter for several years. The interview took place on the veranda of a wooden bungalow three minutes' walk from the tree in Bodh Gaya, where the Buddha was enlightened.

CT: Firstly, I would like to discuss Buddhism in its practical sense. As you know, most Buddhists, particularly in Asia, are born into Buddhism. Perhaps a strong emphasis for them is taking refuge in the triple gem and making of merit through devotion and support of the monks, the *bhikkhu sangha*. There is also a much smaller percentage of people, both *bhikkhus* and lay people, who view Buddhism from a more practical standpoint and therefore include meditation. Would you say, in your observation in Burma especially, that there is an increase of interest in the practice of *vipassana* (insight) meditation?

U NU: Yes, there is, because *vipassana* is the only path that can lead one to emancipation from suffering – that is to say, suffering due to previous rebirths and such concomitants as birth, ageing, sickness, death and separation from dear ones. In the past, the emphasis in Buddhism was laid on *sila* [ethics] and *dana* [generosity and offerings]. *Sila* means refraining from harmful action. In those days *vipassana* was practised alone. The monks who were learned were found to be learned only by the Buddhist texts. *Vipassana* cannot be imparted to another person unless the person who imparts has experienced depths of meditation. So many of the monks who were approached to teach were really helpless. The first important preparation for meditation is observe the *sila*. You take these vows in the presence of the Buddha or in the presence of a monk and very faithfully observe them.

CT: It is quite a step . . .

U NU: Please don't disturb. I have now reached an age where the memory becomes very poor. Sometimes I have even forgotten how to enumerate five precepts. So I have to be very careful what I say as we are engaged in a serious topic. I want to tell you what I know.

The second point is *samadhi*. *Samadhi* means concentration. Unless we have *sila*, we cannot have concentration. Someone with *sila* can concentrate. In the case of *samatha* [calmness], there are two different types of *bhavana* [inner development]: one is *samatha* and the other is *vipassana*. In the case of *vipassana*, the concentration is on yourself. The mind must be aware only of mind and body and must not go out. So long as you acquire steadfast mindfulness on the five *khandas*, [the five aggregates which comprise a human being – namely body, feelings, perceptions, thoughts and consciousness] it is enough. Some people say that it is difficult. It is not difficult. The only thing that you have got to do in *vipassana* meditation is to have steadfast mindfulness on these five *khandas* which make up mind and body.

Don't let the mindfulness go away. For instance, you may find something very delightful, very interesting if the mind goes to meritorious actions of the Buddha, so much so that you have a sudden feeling of reverence for the Buddha so that you then concentrate on that. However, you mustn't do it. In *vipassana*, if you want to find the Path, which is the most important thing in *vipassana*, you must not let your mind go away from yourself, even to focus on the glories of the Buddha.

CT: What is the purpose of the sustained mindfulness . . .

U NU: You are a man who doesn't listen to me. You are disturbing me. [With a smile.] Why are you so impatient? Just listen and then ask questions. Yesterday, I met a Burmese monk. I was asked to give a talk at the International Meditation Centre [in Bodh Gaya]. I tried to enumerate eight precepts. I forgot one of them. I cannot remember them though it is a very easy thing for Buddhists. If you disturb me, let us break the meeting off. I will not be able to continue. Because of my weakness I am making this request to you.

CT: You mentioned how easily we can become attracted to the qualities of the Buddha.

U NU: Don't allow yourself to be attracted to the glories of the Buddha. Attention must be given to the five *khandas*. Many learned people who are well versed in the Buddhist texts come to the meditation centre in Rangoon to practise *vipassana*. As they go on they reach certain points and have experiences which they have never experienced before. Then they start thinking, 'Oh, that is what I have read in a certain section of the texts.' Then these thoughts will start taking them away from concentration on the five *khandas*. If you want to lift this cup, ordinarily you don't know the desire to lift. But when you lift you can know that some mental intention is pushing the hand forward. Unless you realize these intentions you will not realize *anicca* [impermanence]. The mind is not one thing but is made up of different parts which condition other mental parts that are appearing and dying, appearing and dying.

CT: You have emphasized the importance of sustained mindfulness on the five aggregates. You say that this mindfulness enables us to see these sparks of moments coming and going, coming and going.

U NU: Not see, but experience. It is something like this. I am not sure if this example is quite appropriate here. A blind man does not see but when he is walking along the road he knows that he is walking along the road. In this way, one does not actually see the appearance of these mental sparks but one knows that something appears in the mind. You know the appearance of the desire even though you do not actually see the mental spark. As time goes on, the mental concentration grows more stable and steadfast. The desire appears and disappears and so on. When you lift the cup, you lift the cup. But before you lift the cup there must be desire to lift the cup. Another mental spark pushes the hand forward and also expires as soon as the cup has been touched. When you have that step by step mindfulness, you are aware of the mental factors pushing your hand, or anything else, forward little bit by little.

One of the glories of the *dharma* [the teachings of the Buddha] is that the Buddha said those who practise will know the truth from their personal experience. Before you practise you don't know truth and you don't believe that you will know and you will have doubts about the *dharma*. As you practise *vipassana*, you will know in the course of time.

CT: One important aspect of *vipassana* meditation is experiencing the mental factors.

U NU: You experience when a mental factor such as desire is present and when it is not present. For example, you see a diamond ring and then you have the desire for it. When you don't have the desire, you know that you don't have the desire. Do I make myself clear to you?

CT: Yes. Our experiencing of desire is so that we can let go of desires which arise out of greed, anger and delusion. We can allow other desires to follow through. What is the relationship between the desire to give to someone, the desire to have a cup of tea and the desire to work with harmful desires?

U NU: These desires should not be connected. Ordinarily, desires are associated with greed, anger and delusion. But when you are concentrating on the appearance of the desire, then greed, anger and delusion cannot control you.

CT: You would say, therefore, that desire is always related to greed, anger and delusion. And the simple expression of drinking a cup of tea and going towards it without greed, anger or delusion means that there is no desire. It is just an activity?

U NU: Yes. But, of course, there can be greed with regard to getting a cup of tea. You use the word 'always'. Desire is not always associated with greed and anger. An *anagami* [the third stage of spiritual awakening where one is free from any greed or anger] has uprooted attachment to sensual pleasures. Such a person has no desire to harm you or get you into trouble. But an *anagami* has desire – the desire to do good things, the desire to see you well, the desire to see you free from enmity and so on.

CT: You might say that this desire is a very pure form of desire. It is not causing suffering.

U NU: Yes. Quite so. So long as the person has not got to the final stage of liberation, which will uproot *mana* [conceit], he will still experience desire which leads to suffering.

CT: In the fourth stage, desire is eliminated from the mind altogether.

U NU: Yes. In the fourth stage, where one has achieved *arahant*, one even gives up attachment to becoming a *brahma*, to wanting to be one with God. And yet, even the Venerable Sariputtra, [a companion of the Buddha] who had achieved *arahant*, still had some desire. For example, he wanted to see the grounds of the monastery kept clean. Every morning he swept the grounds.

CT: So this desire has a different quality to ordinary desire?

U NU: Ordinary desires are often connected to greed, anger and delusion. As for these other desires, these are quite different. They are devoid of defilements.

CT: So we have mentioned that *vipassana* practice helps us to experience the *khandas* more clearly . . .

U NU: The first thing you must have is *sila*. The second thing you must have is mental concentration through mindfulness of the five *khandas*. This concentration is called *samadhi*. From *sila* and *samadhi* comes *panna*, or wisdom. In my case I wanted to know the wonders I would get by practising *vipassana*. I wanted to know whether by meditation alone I can uproot greed and anger. I wondered, can it be true? I had heard such things. When we enter the presence of the meditation centre with the desire to practise *vipassana* meditation, we are filled with defilements. The faith of a person with defilements cannot be said to be strong. There may also be some fear that the person will be reborn in one of the hell realms. We sit and practise the four foundations for awareness, namely awareness of body, feelings, mental states and *dharma*, as laid down by the Buddha. As soon as one of the parts of the body moves, you must know it. As soon as you feel pain or happy or sad, you know what you are feeling. *Vipassana* is that you know. If you have sexual desire, you must know that you have sexual desire. You must know at once the kind of mind you have in the moment. You must not welcome any kind of thoughts. As soon as you have thoughts, you must know you have thoughts. The thoughts will stop. If the mindfulness is not so steadfast, it will get into greed and anger and so forth. You must learn to stop your mind from wandering into these nets of greed and anger.

As soon as you truly know you have anger, the anger stops at that particular moment; you know you have anger but you have no desire in that mind moment. One mind moment has only one content present in it. So long as you are aware when feelings, mental states or trains of thoughts appear you will have mental concentration. But it is not *just* a mental concentration. When you are meditating to be relaxed and calm it is a different kind of concentration. You can be aware of anything that pertains to the body as soon as it appears. If you have any feeling, as soon as it appears you know it. Similarly, with any type of mind state or thought. You will see the true nature of the five *khandas* – that they are impermanent, unsatisfactory and not self [no possessor]. You must be aware. If you are not aware, you are off track.

CT: Can a person be happy with this condition?

U NU: When the perception of impermanence, or unsatisfactoriness, is seen through observing the continuous crumbling of the mental states and bodily sensations, I don't think any reasonable person can be happy about it. 'Oh, my mind and body.' This is *dukkha* [unsatisfactoriness].

If you go about such observation, you will know *anatta* [impersonal or not-self] as the Buddha taught. He said there is no such thing as a soul. Someone might say they have a soul which is directing them to do this and that. Without trying in the least, realizations about mind/body dawn upon them in meditation. If the totality of mind/body is impermanent it cannot be said to have a 'self' or a soul which is permanent. Physical sensations and mental sparks are crumbling continuously. The identification with the process of mind/body from the very beginning of *samsara* [the wheel of rebirth] up to the present ceases when there is realization. We practise to develop *sila*, *samadhi* and *panna* until there is realization.

Life is a pearl

An interview with Fleana Bergonzi
Rome, Italy

At the present time, one in five people in the Western world will at some time be diagnosed with cancer. Both allopathic medicine and alternative therapies are working to combat this disease. Given the hectic pace in the Western world, it is not surprising that some of the contributing factors to cancer appear to be pollution, diet and stress.

I first met Fleana Bergonzi's son, Mauro, a student of oriental philosophies and religions at Rome University who had participated in a number of Buddhist retreats. He was translating various texts on Eastern spirituality from English to Italian, thereby contributing to the increase in peoples' understanding of Eastern wisdom. One of the books he translated was *Experience of Insight*, by Joseph Goldstein, an insight meditation teacher. Both Mauro and, later, his mother practised insight meditation in Italy with Corrado Pensa, a professor at Rome University.

Fleana, a mother and housewife, told me that she became quite interested in what her son was involved in. She observed, too, that the process of meditation and self-observation was making noticeable changes in his consciousness. So she asked him to give her meditation instructions.

Some years previously, she had two separate operations which removed both breasts. She felt certain that the cancer would not return but ten years later, in 1982, it did. It was at this time that she asked Mauro to teach her meditation; by now he had years of exposure to the practice. In order to expand her self-understanding even more she started to meet regularly with a psychotherapist.

In some parts of the Western world, there is still a widespread view, and it is largely misinformed, that anyone who visits a psychotherapist regularly must be either neurotic, depressed, trapped in a phobia or suicidal. Certainly, a therapist works with such clients,

but for many who are well-adjusted to daily life, the regular meeting
with the therapist is an opportunity to deal with personal pain and
to find out more about oneself. The therapist has a valuable role
to play in this regard.

By 1983, she knew she was experiencing a life-threatening illness
and it was only a matter of time before the cancer consumed the
whole organism. The cancer began to move fast and was carried
to the brain.

Mauro and another friend, Francesca Rusciani (who acted as an
interpreter) went with me to his parents' home, a spacious apartment in Montesacro, one of the countless suburbs of Rome. Not
only was the family dealing with the cancer, but also the possibility
of having to move from this rented accommodation. Finding somewhere to live in Rome can be a nightmarish business.

The five of us, including Fleana's husband, Egiolio, sat down to a
lunch of pasta and wine. We began speaking together in generalities
about Rome, the Pope, the weather and mutual friends. From there
we began to explore the impact the cancer had, not only on the
family, but also on the neighbours with whom the Bergonzi's
seemed to have a rather easy-going relationship.

Fleana was as talkative as the rest of us. The only visible sign of
her illness was that she had lost most of her hair due to radiation
treatments. She was relaxed, attentive and more than willing to
share her experiences. She exemplified what in some circles would
be called an 'open system'. At the dinner table, her husband said
very little except to expand or clarify a point from time to time. I
could tell from his eyes that he was immensely proud of the dignity
and clarity his wife had in dealing with this pervasive cancer.

Later in the day, Fleana and I sat down together in the living
room and I recorded the interview with her, exploring the general
history of the cancer and her relationship to the events. A number
of times there were tears in her eyes as she recalled an event from
her past. There was a precious quietness as the meeting flowed on.

One of the thoughts I had during the interview was whether or
not the clarity and expansive understanding which Fleana had then
would be able to carry her through the more advanced stages of
the cancer.

Twelve months after the interview Fleana died. Mauro telephoned me from Rome. I asked him how she had coped with the
last weeks and days. He told me that she was even more radiant

and serene than the day I spent with her. She had died with 'an innocent smile'.

CT: Could you tell me about the history of the cancer?

FB: It started when I was 38 years old when I had the left breast taken away. At that time I felt a sense of rebellion and victimization. Eight years later, I had an operation on the right breast. My reaction was very bad; I felt a lot of fear, endless fear. Three years ago, when I was 56, the cancer came back through metastasis at the bones. [Metastasis is a cancer which starts somewhere else and spreads everywhere including the brain. Clumps of cells break off from the original mass and are carried by lymphatic vessels or the blood stream to distant parts of the body.] The same thing had happened to my mother. So many people around me were dying of cancer. Because of all this, I started to understand that something new should happen in my life so I went to seek help because I felt that on my own I couldn't succeed. I couldn't go on living with so much fear and pain. A great help has come from my son, Mauro, who has been trained in Eastern philosophy and religion. He taught me to meditate. And there have been other wonderful people who have been really helpful to me through their love and affection.

CT: Three years ago, did you expect the cancer to return?

FB: After two operations on the breast, I thought that the cancer had gone for ever. So for ten years I felt sure in myself that I needn't worry about it anymore. The doctors then told me that a metastasis of the cancer had taken place. There was nothing else to be done. The cancer had spread everywhere. Here and there. All the back bones, ribs and brain.

CT: How much physical pain was there?

FB: At the beginning, the pain was very, very strong. I could hardly move. I can remember some days when the pain was really intense. Doctors are often not very clear. They do not say very much about what's really going on. So at the beginning my husband, son and I spoke a lot between us about accepting the situation and coping with it. But, the doctor that I'm seeing now is very clear. We had a good talk together. He told me that a metastasis of the cancer had taken place and that I had to take certain medicines, hormones. So I started to take them and the pain has decreased.

CT: At that time, what were you experiencing inside of yourself?

FB: Something new was starting to take place in my life. I had been in a meditation group for some time with my son and friends that I was close to. I can say that through this community, through certain books I read, through the care and love of my friends, I really jumped to another dimension. By then, I had already gone to see a psychotherapist who was also interested in working with cancer through a method influenced by Simonton's therapy.

CT: What was the original reason for going to the psycho-therapist?

FB: I needed help to go through life and face death.

CT: What kind of meditation were you doing?

FB: Vipassana (insight) meditation which works with the breath and body scanning. While doing the body scanning I used to stop in the areas which were most painful. I used to wait for the pain to melt down, or to move, or sometimes, to become a knot. In the end, the pain used to dissolve. Then it would come back. Generally speaking, I had great benefit from the meditation. I started looking for a physical benefit and I found a great spiritual richness. I realized the most important thing was to make every day a full day, a full and alive day. Psychologically speaking, the benefit I got was very great. What I learned is that the body and mind go very much together.

CT: So this became a spiritual concern affecting your relationship to life?

FB: Definitely. I just want to live everyday as an end in itself, a treasure. I would think this before I began meditation, but then as I went on meditating I began to understand this in a much deeper way. I started to see myself from an external point of observation, as if I were detached from myself and was able to see how many useless pains and passions there are in life, and I started to feel more detached from all that.

CT: Was this feeling of being detached from everything a feeling of alienation or seeing more clearly?

FB: It was definitely positive detachment, to see my projections, my dreams and fantasies.

CT: In the therapy, were you concentrating on any area of your life, such as the relationship to yourself or to someone else?

FB: At the beginning, the psychotherapist and I began to look with care at what had happened in the periods of time just before the first two operations. The psychotherapist asked why I allowed cancer to grow in myself? I told him I felt like a martyr and a saint. I suffered a lot when my husband lost his job. I felt hurt by a great sense of humiliation. All my life I have been helping others with a somehow blind sense of self-mortification, without really taking care of myself. So whenever I happened to suffer in life, I did not feel any responsibility for what was going on; I thought it was an external accident which had nothing to do with me, so I had to bear it patiently, surrounded by a halo of sanctity. I thought I was extremely righteous; absolute honesty and morality were my favourite virtues. Everything had to be perfect in me, especially as a wife and mother.

CT: And what did the cancer tell you?

FB: That it was all wrong.

CT: It sounds like the combination of therapy and meditation was quite essential for you in that period.

FB: It gave me the possibility to see life and other people through different eyes. First, we began working with the relationship to the cancer and the operations. Then together we inquired very deeply into my childhood, especially my relationship with my parents and the problems that I had as an illegitimate child. Then we inquired further into more recent problems, for example, being like a puppet with a mask on my face all the time. Through therapy I could gradually see certain images of myself and of my life collapse, leaving a free space.

CT: Let me get the picture right. In your childhood you were cut off from yourself, hence the mask image. The way that this manifested as an adult was by cutting yourself off from yourself by being lost in other people.

FB: Yes, definitely.

CT: So you went into meditation and therapy. What did you do next?

FB: I tried to find new interests in life. For example, I had no plants or flowers in my house, and now my home [her eyes were filling with tears] is full of plants and flowers.

CT: Do you know about how many you have?

FB: Dozens, plus six small trees outside.

CT: The cancer is still present and you are replacing it with new life around you.

FB: Yes, that is true. It is like there is a workshop inside of me where I have the most pain. And from that place – especially when pain melts down – a lot of compassion comes: compassion for me, for others, for anybody who is suffering. It is a workshop where pain and fear turn into love for every single being who is suffering. And I feel surrounded by lots of love.

CT: Did you practise and apply the Simonton method of meditation, using visualization?

FB: Yes, my therapist helped me learn the method. I practised the visualizations and in doing so, lots of memories that I had completely forgotten about came up, and also lots of insights.

CT: Did the strong memories have any impact on the body?

FB: Yes. I can remember an image of my mother when she was very young and beautiful. That image gave me great happiness and also physical strength.

CT: Why did the image give you that? You said that your mother died from cancer.

FB: Up to that moment, the image which had remained in my mind was of my mother being sick and weak, needing help which I was unable to give her. So a fresh image of my mother – young, beautiful and full of strength – gave me strength in myself as well.

CT: Very important. As you came fully into the present, you brought more life into your home, as expressed through the plants. That transformation also transformed your memory.

FB: Yes. The image of that unhappy, weak sick child that I was has dissolved without giving me any more problems.

CT: As you see more life in the present, you see more life in the past.

FB: Yes, it's like that. And I found again all the beautiful things in the past that I hadn't been able to appreciate. In one of my visualizations I saw very clearly the little child I was, so much suffering – unhappy, ailing and unhealthy, not only physically but also emotionally. She was dying. In order to be sure that she was really dying, that she was finally going away from my mind I looked closely through her open mouth and saw her atrophic heart and liver. Deeply relieved, I said, 'She's dead. At long last!'

CT: Seeing that this suffering child of the past was now gone, how did that affect your relationship to life, your cancer and the present?

FB: I have grown up into love and appreciation for a human being's face, for a little animal, for whatever.

CT: You told me earlier how you had given your life to others and neglected yourself considerably. Yet you still had love and compassion for others. What is the difference between now and the time when you thought of yourself as a martyr or saint?

FB: There is a very great difference. Before there was a sense of duty. Now there is joy.

CT: An extraordinary awareness. The present is an expression of effortlessness and spontaneity with a foundation of joy. Whereas, previously, doing good came from a compelling factor. The cancer is still present; it hasn't actually stopped. What is the doctor telling you now about your physical condition?

FB: I haven't asked the doctor. I feel that for each person the experience of cancer can be quite different. So there is not much point to ask doctors for a forecast. The doctors can say what medicine you can take and what treatment you can go on, but they can't tell you what the future is going to be.

CT: I would like to explore further these important experiences which you have had. You might call them 'spiritual' experiences. Did these occur mostly when there was a lot of pain, or did they occur in meditation?

FB: Firstly, in meditation, especially during retreats. Things that I had been wondering about and asking myself all my life finally came to a clarification, to an understanding – the relationship with the earth, the flowers, the plants, with life itself which is flowing from moment to moment, feeling enchanted by seeing a laurel tree and its leaves, feeling deeply touched by the wonder of it. I felt the difference between mere living and feeling alive, feeling life flowing within myself, being one with the earth, with the rose, with plants and flowers.

One time during a walk, I happened to fall down and as soon as my face touched the earth, there was a moment of great communion: I felt I was the earth itself and I was its smell; I was the flowers around me; I was the bird which was filling my whole inner space with its twittering; I was the tree and everything else.

Another time, I realized our life is a pearl. But this could take place only after passing through a kind of agony full of crying and sobbing, which was painful and sweet at the same time. By sobbing, I was preparing the ground, the shell for the pearl to take birth. At that time I thought I was going to die. I was preparing a kind of shell inside myself, without knowing why. When I saw a pearl taking birth in it, the sobbing settled down, the pearl melted itself, it became a single tear, and I realized that it was my whole life. I saw my son's eyes and Corrado's eyes melting together into one light, an immeasurable sweetness surrounded me and I felt one with God.

CT: Why, at that time, did you think that you were going to die?

FB: I was tired and I thought it was time to die.

CT: After seeing the pearl dissolve into a tear and then dissolve into God, was there any relationship of that experience to the cancer?

FB: I felt that the cancer was a light which had brought me to that point. I owed it my understanding. I was feeling very thankful to the cancer. [Tears in her eyes.] The illness has given me this possibility. I feel thankful for all the good opportunities which life has given me: the meditation, the therapy, the people that I have met, the readings.

CT: You have had cancer since your late thirties. You experience its reoccurrence and it is now brain cancer. There is a transformation of a totally life-threatening situation and it has become an instrument for life affirmation. You have gone from fear to gratitude.

FB: The love comes free and surrounds me at the most difficult and most painful moments. For example, when my mind was dull and confused because of the brain cancer and radiation treatment, I would wake up early in the morning at about 5 a.m. and waves of tenderness caught me and tears flew out of my eyes without knowing why: sweet, very sweet tears. Then I used to think of all the people that were dying, or wanted to die but couldn't. I would think of all the people who felt they were not loved. Then I tried with all my heart to send them love, so that they could feel this love that surrounds all of us, this love which is freely available and comes to us as a benediction if only we let ourselves go.

CT: You are saying that the resistance and conflict with the cancer is emotionally and psychologically dropping away so that love can manifest?

FB: In the times that I was seriously ill and keeping my attention on the breath, I used to hear a call in my bed that said, 'Go beyond, go beyond.' This voice gave me a great sense of freedom of getting over every limited space.

CT: Presumably there are still fears.

FB: I couldn't describe them; there may be moments of uneasiness, restlessness. Corrado once asked me, 'Fleana, are you afraid?' I straight away answered no, but then I spent the whole following day and night inquiring into that. I haven't been able to describe a real fear. Maybe there is still some fear somewhere. I'll see it when it comes.

CT: How much radiation treatment have you had?

FB: So far I've had twenty-five applications. A machine works with radiation in a very precise area of my head. The radiation has been applied to the brain which is the reason why I have often felt dull and confused. Sometimes I see double vision. I think it is possible to have some kind of awareness even if your mind is confused. I felt very much close to the Hiroshima victims when I lost all my hair because of the radiation. I felt close to the deep suffering of all those people.

CT: Even with the radiation, the pain, the confusion, there is still an awareness that is transcendent and a sympathy with the whole of life. Have the doctors expressed an opinion about the amount of pain you experience?

FB: Actually, the doctor assessed that I should have severe pains in my bones. But I don't feel such pains. He was very surprised and couldn't understand it. I couldn't understand it at first, either. But now, it seems to me natural that I don't feel such pain. For two years, I have been putting a lot of energy on awareness of pain. Firstly, I send feelings of love and compassion to Fleana. Then to the pain, from the pain to everybody else and out to the whole universe. The support I have has really been essential. One day in my visualization meditation my son was revealed to me as my biggest medicine. My husband, although he is an old man, has done things I have never seen him do before: shopping, cooking, taking care of the bedroom, taking care of me. He'll take me anywhere I need to go. The whole of his life is totally devoted to me.

My neighbours have been doing incredible things for me, too. I've been very sick for the past four months. My neighbours have been like a very well-organized community in their visits. Although they never talk about organizing the visits, everything seems to just come naturally. They are always leaving dishes of food and offering us any kind of support. One lady – I don't know her very well – is a prostitute. One day, she sent me a wonderful plant of hydrangeas and a big bunch of yellow roses. Then she came with a kind of childlike shyness and we embraced each other.

CT: Your life, love and warmth seems to be attracting life, love and warmth.

FB: I believe this.

CT: In what ways has Mauro been a support to you?

FB: Well, for example, I was sitting on the toilet and I was so weak I couldn't stand up. Mauro helped me to stand up to go to my bedroom. When I had to have the radiation he would take me there every time. I have learnt meditation from him and he has introduced me to his friends.

CT: I'm feeling very touched and nourished by this whole experience with you. We cannot feel your pain when it arises but we can feel, within ourselves, your love. Finally, how do you regard the future?

FB: The future is tomorrow. I hope that it will be a nice day. I hope that we will be able to go out and have a walk. I shall see what I shall find tomorrow. It will be a surprise. I might find a blossomed tree, or meet somebody. I'll just see what comes. Every day brings me something new.

CT: There is the reality of cancer, and the reality of the transcendent which embraces the cancer and allows you to see so much more. Everything you have said to us this afternoon is a wonderful testimony to what is possible in the face of suffering. We very much appreciate your willingness to look back over these past years with us.

FB: The richness that I am feeling comes from beyond and is nourishing me. And this richness belongs to everybody.

CT: That is a beautiful point to finish on. Thank you.

ATTITUDES TOWARD CREATURES AND PLANET

The crisis is here now

An interview with Jonathon Porritt
London, England

Jonathon Porritt comes from a privileged background. He is one of the seven per cent of British children who go to private instead of state schools. He went to Eton and from there to Oxford University where he obtained a degree in Modern Languages.

When he was 18 years old, his parents bought some land in New Zealand which had the name Rangitopuni. Jonathon went there to plant pine trees on the land in well-ordered rows. It was through this experience that he developed a deep relationship with the environment. Nearby was a five-acre patch of land which somehow escaped the attention of the developers. This was called 'The Cathedral', since there the native trees soar up like the nave of a cathedral; below, it is hushed. There, Jonathon says, 'Songs of praise are silently uttered.' He says, 'I have learned that wildness abounds far beyond the ever-shrinking confines of wilderness. There is wildness in your own back yard, in your garden or somewhere down your favourite walk, even in your window box, but only if there is wildness in your soul.'

During years of teaching in a school in West London, he became increasingly interested in the fledgling Ecology Party, as it was then called. His presence in the party was quickly felt. He became an articulate campaigner on green issues and within a few years was one of the chairpersons. The party is now re-named the Green Party.

Generally speaking, the kind of educational upbringing and background that Jonathon had is regarded as being more suitable for conventional politics or entering the fields of industry, commerce or the civil service, but he chose none of those areas. As an Ecology Party candidate, he stood on seven occasions in local, European and general elections. In September 1984, *Seeing Green* was published, a book in which Jonathon provides the general reader with a clear explanation of the politics of ecology. Following its widespread success, Jonathon made regular appearances on television, radio and numerous public platforms, establishing him as a leading spokesperson for the Green movement. He gave up teaching to concentrate full-time on ecological issues and was appointed Director of Friends of the Earth.

Now based in London, he can be seen at times pedalling his way around town, and to and from work. He acknowledges that his life, like that of other committed people, leaves little time for aloneness and reflection, which he admits 'matters enormously'. He was once giving a public talk at Sharpham House in Ashprington, a community close to where I live. Prior to the talk there was a 45-minute silent meditation and afterwards Jonathon told the audience that it was the first time in four or five months that he had the opportunity to experience that quality of silence.

The interview with Jonathon took place in his office, which is a small room on the top of Friends of the Earth's old building in London. We explored some of the moral and ethical principles facing the politics of ecology today.

CT: In the very last passage of *Seeing Green* you say, 'Stripped of a spiritual dimension, politics in today's world is a hollow shell, and religion stripped of its political dimension is irresponsibly escapist.' What do you mean by 'spiritual'?

JP: I suspect that I kept the definition as loose and open as possible because one of the central principles of Green thinking is the acknowledgement and recognition of diversity. If you start to define things too closely you start to exclude people by virtue of the narrowness of the terms that you are relying on. It has also been part of my understanding not to narrow down that concept to any one interpretation. But that approach can be criticized because of a lack of intellectual rigour, or indeed, a lack of spiritual integrity, if you are not prepared to specify what you mean by the word. To me, the word has a meaning that is quite clear. I have always used it to refer to that aspect of human nature that allows people to transcend the limitations of their material world, to seek meaning in that which cannot be defined materialistically or scientifically.

CT: There *is* the need to transcend materialistic ambitions through concern for the planet. On the other hand, all too often there can be neglect of the quality of one's own life.

JP: Yes, though I doubt that's true of most people in Green organizations today. I believe that people think very carefully about the quality of their life. They think carefully about what they eat, how they travel, the clothes they wear; whether they are wasting things; whether they are dealing with people the way they should be; are they becoming victims of a consumer society? However, it would not necessarily be true to say that such a lifestyle concern always embraces a spiritual dimension. People aren't necessarily thinking day-to-day about what it is that makes life good and what keeps us from trespassing too heavily on the planet. But I have been impressed over the years by a significant proportion of people in the Green movement that do feel a spiritual dimension in their lives as well as the quality of life dimension. Unless our way of life actually does reflect our political beliefs and our philosophical position, then it's barely worth puting those beliefs and that position down on paper. Everything we do impinges directly on the lifestyle and quality of life of people in this country and in other countries.

But for me that would not wholly define the spiritual dimension. There are many people in the Green movement who would show this concern for the quality of life and yet who would dismiss as irrelevant any further thoughts about what the spirit is that underlies their decisions, actions and ethics. They would quite clearly distinguish between an ethical position and a spiritual one.

CT: What kind of criterion is at work to say this is an ethical or a spiritual position?

JP: Spiritual would include ethical but ethical doesn't necessarily include the spiritual. Ethically, for instance, people in the Green movement would say it is not acceptable to go on using the Earth's resources in such a way as to deny two-thirds of humanity the right to exist with any dignity or decency. If this is your position then the moral consequence is that you have changed your lifestyle accordingly to accommodate that moral principle. But they wouldn't necessarily link that to any spiritual attitude or any other religious or metaphysical concerns. It would be wrong to say that everybody in the Green movement is concerned about the spiritual dimension. But there are a large number who are concerned. It's a question I think of taking those moral, ethical and ecological principles and seeing whether one finds something that embraces them all in a different and deeper way. To me, for instance, one must acknowledge the truly radical meaning of that very simple phrase – to live in harmony with the Earth – and make that possible and feasible. I actually think that you need a spiritual relationship with the Earth. I do not think it is possible to achieve such harmony in a purely utilitarian, functional way.

CT: Are your equating here the utilitarian aspect with voluntary simplicity?

JP: Well, not necessarily. Because again, there are people who follow the principles of voluntary simplicity who would do so to uphold the quality of life for as many people as possible but not necessarily for any deeper spiritual concerns. To take a classic divide within the Green movement, there is a real ethical dilemma as to whether we look upon humankind as being a part of creation – a biocentric view – or whether we see humankind as separate from the rest of creation. The latter position has dominated the development of society and civilization for the last four or five hundred years and has led to what I consider to be almost an entirely anthropocentric view of life. The former position was certainly held predominantly by what are referred to as 'primitive people' who are in the web of life rather than apart from it. Now, for me, the anthropocentric vision of man (and I mean 'man' rather than 'human'!) is of a dominant dominion rather than a caring, responsible stewardship. A biocentric view of life needs to be interpreted in a more spiritual way.

CT: One may speak of a 'primitive' culture but, of course, there are other biocentric philosophies. The Buddhist philosophy and practice is about this relationship of the individual to life.

JP: That's right. With Buddhism, one finds an entirely different pattern emerging that has little to do with the dominant strands of philosophy and thought in our society.

CT: In many respects, our Western society has created a separation from the planet through a massive degree of control over the environment.

JP: Yes. Some people in the Green movement say that the anthropocentric view of life is correct and that all we need to do is to manage our resources more efficiently. Essentially, what they are saying is that utilitarian principles are not fundamentally incorrect but that they have just not been operating as efficiently as they might be. In that context, when one is talking about a more conservationist-orientated approach to life, what we are really talking about is managing that resource more efficiently so that it meets the need of many people for a longer period of time.

For example, from a utilitarian approach, once whale populations are restored to something like their former size, we can sustain a certain amount of whale hunting every year. There are some people who would say that it's legitimate to continue to hunt the whales sustainably from here to the end of time – taking so many per year so as not to damage the breeding population. There are other people who would say that the whole ethic is false; that the very notion of a sustainable use which requires the destruction of the whales, or any other species, is flawed philosophically and is not worth considering. I hold to the latter position very strongly. One of the problems is that much of the writing, and often the thought, that goes into the environmental movement today is still completely trapped by utilitarian principles.

CT: Is it more than just a philosophical viewpoint or is such questioning actually affecting people's action?

JP: I think it's beginning to have an effect. Take the animal rights movement. Fifteen to twenty years ago the animal rights movement was seen as little more than a gathering of elderly animal lovers. Today animal rights is an important part of radical thought. We are asking, 'What kind of relationship do we want with animals?' There is a much stronger philosophical awareness of what it is that justifies or invalidates the cause. We are challenged philosophically.

CT: There is a real urgency for this kind of questioning – more than four million animals are experimented upon and killed in British laboratories each year.

JP: Yes. In the past, a lot of issues would have been dealt with at the level of superficial, political responses with people saying, 'This policy will sort this out.' That approach is no longer adequate. It's now necessary to look at things from a deeper perspective and say, 'Not only have we got to do this, here are the reasons why.' We have to look at our *relationship* to life on Earth. Unless we get that relationship right philosophically, it is unlikely we'll get the policies enforced that would match up with that relationship.

CT: Contemporary social–political patterns appeal very, very strongly to self-interest. The message has to go out to people to take responsibility for poverty, violence, cancer, and unhappiness in the West, and elsewhere. I sometimes get concerned when we speak of a *future* crisis. In my observation, the crisis has already arrived. Genuine self-interest and global interest is the same.

JP: Yes, it's here now. It's not as if we should be sheepish in arguing about a new enlightened form of self-interest. The need to be out there, putting that to people is crucial. On every page of the Brundtland Report [a 1987 report dealing with economic development and global change], you find justification for why we should help the Third World in order to build up *our* markets, increase *our* exports, develop relationships we haven't had before. 'Do this and you'll benefit in the long run. And if you don't, watch out, because things are going to be bad.'

No doubt people would say the Brundtland Report was imbued with an ethic of enlightened self-interest. I would say it's a very limited form of self-interest, and 'enlightened' only in as much as it's based on the assumption that the Third World benefits economically only if we build up our markets in the developed world. The report still fails to go beyond the constraints of a materialistic interpretation of self-interest. If we talk more in terms of personal rather than economic growth, we can give people a clearer interpretation of what 'self-interest' might really mean.

CT: The phrase 'personal growth' is very much in the rhetoric. It isn't going to mean much to someone who lives in a high-rise apartment.

JP: It genuinely depends. There is so much alienation and unhappiness that to talk of personal growth, without perhaps, using that phrase, certainly shouldn't be seen as elitist or irrelevant. There are ways of trying to enrich people's lives without necessarily exploiting the finite wealth of the planet.

CT: Yes. The degree of alienation is so great – people alienated from each other, from animals, from the Earth. We have a long history of being removed – physically, psychologically, emotionally and spiritually. What is going to breach this separation?

JP: That's the crunch.

CT: That *is* the crunch, isn't it? There is the fact of alienation. How is that fact going to reach people's hearts?

JP: It depends on how you look at this. The Americans are wonderfully optimistic about it all. They use this wonderful phrase, 'the quantum leap', which refers to millions of people suddenly reaching a new plane of awareness. The French are quite the opposite. They say there is this gap and we'll never bridge it, so let's just talk about what it would have been like if we had bridged it! Very depressing. I think that in the UK there is a rather more sanguine realism about this situation and the problems of bridging that gap.

Something that is indirectly enhancing our ability to get our message across is that all other messages are being revealed as increasingly empty and incapable of meeting people's needs, even their material needs. Some of the political promises that underpinned our life have ceased to have a lot of meaning. More positively, however, people have begun to look to other options. For example, not everybody today considers unemployment to be a scourge. Many people today look at unemployment as an opportunity to develop potentialities that could simply not have been expressed before. So people are taking the negative and seeing the positive side.

CT: People easily get burnt out, experience frustration, and a loss of energy and focus. To some extent, this characterises what is happening to society – feelings of hopelessness and helplessness. How do you guard against this?

JP: It's very difficult. People in the Green movement are just as vulnerable to either that sense of exhaustion, spiritual and physical, or indeed, to the gradual erosion of compromise, whereby people's principles are thinned out by virtue of their confrontation with reality. Those who don't base their convictions exclusively in political principles, but feel that the spiritual dimension is very important, seem to have a deeper reserve that they're able to call on. And this seems to remain intact even when they are being assailed by all kinds of depressing views and difficult questions about whether they are doing the right thing. If there is that spiritual reserve, it gives you a sense of purpose that simply lets you pass over lots of negativity in a way that you don't think you could have otherwise. I know that I would not have been in Green politics for ten years if I hadn't felt very strongly the sense of spiritual commitment that lies behind it, not just the personal political commitment – although I don't much like to separate those things out. I've been one of those who have reasoned for integration of spiritual and political life for a very long time. I am convinced that the ideas will never establish themselves fast enough and thoroughly enough exclusively through a political process. There is an enormous weight of inertia built into our society which is too great to overcome without a deeper appeal to people's spiritual values. The spiritual dimension has enriched my own life, but it's also provided a backdrop for my political activities. For me, the link between politics and spirituality, as you quoted right from the start, is very close. I'm not really able, in my own mind, to separate them out. The writings of someone like Thomas Merton, for instance, have always made an infinitely greater impact on me than someone capable of skating over any political consequences of their spiritual beliefs.

CT: Now a fly on the wall in this room might say,

JP: There probably is – MI5. (*Laughter*)

CT: One might say, you've either got spiritual awareness or you haven't.

JP: I don't think so. I would disagree with that very profoundly on the basis of my personal experience. I have developed a feeling of reverence for the Earth and creation; I wasn't born with that. I never had it. I was brought up in a city and I used to muck around on Hampstead Heath, but I never actually felt any kind of relationship or 'kinship' (to use a dangerous word!) with the Earth. And it's only gradually, bit by bit, over the years that I've begun to develop a tremendous sense of being bonded with the Earth. I also don't think that I have had any special revelations with regards to more conventional theological or spiritual matters. I'm a blundering, completely incompetent, hopelessly unorthodox Christian when it comes to many things; I'm someone who is fascinated by Eastern mystical traditions; I am a uselessly eclectic hotch-potch when it comes to a spiritual base. What's important is an understanding of the transcendent *in life* – not a million miles removed from ordinary people. I get tetchy when people say we need to be precise about what spirituality is. As soon as you are more precise, you are into laying down what *the* green model of the spirit should be.

CT: Once one endeavours through language to articulate the spiritual, it imposes a set of ideas on it. Yet we must recognize that spirituality includes a deep reverence for life. The Eastern traditions offer meditative ways and means for an inner spiritual renewal to take place. I've felt within the Green movement that there is not sufficient emphasis in that direction.

JP: I think you're right. There are a lot of people in the Green movement who are worried about the spiritual emphasis. Some genuinely feel that it is elitist to talk about spiritual matters – if you combine your political beliefs with your spiritual concerns, you are likely to be setting yourself above the vast mass of humanity and therefore, be less effective politically. I find this to be an extraordinary perception!

CT: The ego can very much identify with the spiritual and create an elitist and superior attitude. One who converts to any view or position is vulnerable to that kind of expression of one's ego through a certain arrogance or conceit that 'I know.'

JP: I can't claim to be immune from that. I am conscious that, on occasion, the way in which I will argue about the link between politics and spirituality is quite dangerously egotistical.

CT: The very awareness of that is probably the major safeguard. If you are discussing the political and the spiritual, people can hear it more easily when you say, 'Yes, I have an interest in this and my ego does get in on the act as well.'

JP: I think it's important for each person to distinguish between the egotistical and the spiritual. For me, the time when I started to think deeply about the animist tradition, which has become an important part of my spirituality, began when I started planting trees in New Zealand. By and large, I got into that for good old capitalist reasons. My parents had bought up some 70 acres of land and they said the trees would be worth a lot of money in the year 2000. And I thought, 'Jolly good idea.' So I was out there in the wind and the rain planting trees, and I can't say that I felt anything deep stirring within me, apart from the fact that I was engaged in a useful activity that I happened to enjoy. But after three or four years, I began to develop a much deeper relationship with those trees and that land. It could have been there from the start had I been open to it, but frankly, I wasn't. Now I'm in a peculiar position of feeling spiritually very close to that piece of land and not very interested in the financial implications of it.

CT: In that respect, we've come full cycle into the transcendence of the material.

JP: That's right. I am encouraged by the extent to which people *can* change even if they are closed off from things. Most people have not chosen this but gradually they have had options and potentials taken away from them. Most people don't actually understand the ways in which their lives are being impoverished in non-material ways. When you read an author like Jeremy Seabrook, for instance, he writes a lot about changes in working class culture and impoverishment of many different kinds, including the damage done to our culture by a loss of direct participation in the arts.

CT: Now just to go back for a moment, you referred to your experience in New Zealand and obviously, this period of time has had an impact on you. To some degree, these types of experience influence the course of one's life, but few people have either the time or opportunity to have that kind of access.

JP: I know. It's difficult to make any sort of response to that because I'm conscious of having had, as you have, an extremely privileged opportunity to be alone in contact with nature. For the most part, I don't reflect a great deal in my daily life; I'm usually very busy and don't have much extra time, which is one of the things that most upsets me. But to be alone for three months or so, which I have done now on four or five occasions, has mattered enormously. Without those periods, I honestly don't think I could sustain the things that I do now. But again, that is a privilege. Where do people find access to solitude in our society today? One is either lonely or overcrowded. The two things seem to cancel each other out.

CT: Solitude can be found by participating in meditation retreats and workshops, or getting out to the countryside. I love my visits to London, although I don't come very often. There is a dynamic energy here with so much to be discovered in the people, the buildings, the parks.

JP: Yes. We are never immune from the power of the Earth.

CT: But so often we want to separate the city from the Earth.

JP: I know someone who I would consider to be in closer contact with the Earth than I'm ever likely to be. He lives in London and has access to one small allotment. And yet, I would say his relationship with the Earth is as rich and as beautiful as anything that anybody could aspire to. He makes no fuss or nonsense about it, and he's not particularly interested in theoretical abstractions about his relationship with the Earth. He simply lives it.

CT: And in that respect, 'Small *is* beautiful.' Thank you.

The silent sufferers

An interview with Jean Pink
London, England

Two hundred thousand animals per year are used in Britain for experiments for cancer research, including grafting and chemically inducing tumours in healthy animals.

A goat's udder is transplanted from its normal biological location to its neck.

Rats are fed massive doses of hair colourants, equivalent to a woman drinking twenty-five bottles of hair colourants in a day.

More than 550 million animals and birds are killed in British abattoirs every year to feed consumers.

In 1978, by picking up a library book, Jean Pink became involved in animals rights. She founded Animal Aid and indirectly spurred other animal rights organizations into concerted action.

As the interview reveals, there is no doubting Jean Pink's sustained commitment to spirituality, which has been a constant thread throughout her life. Married with two adopted children (now adults), Jean Pink is 53, and has spent much of her working life as a primary school teacher. In the mid-1970s she taught at the Hadlow Primary School, two miles from Tonbridge in Kent, an area known for the support of establishment values. Through her decision to follow up her concerns for the welfare of animals, widespread protests – about vivisection throughout Britain and overseas – eventually took place. 'Animals cannot speak for themselves. They depend on human beings to speak for them,' says Jean.

I remember once participating in a demonstration in Salisbury, a West Country town. Thousands of marchers, mostly women, marched through the High Street, under the watchful eye of the police, to a unified shout, 'What do we want? Animal Liberation!

When do we want it? NOW!' At the end of the march, the protestors gathered together in the local park for a rally. Jean gave a speech and the march continued on to Porton Down, where the military conduct some of the most horrific experiments on animals, (and sometimes on human volunteers), for the testing of chemical weapons.

On another occasion I was speaking at the annual general meeting of Animal Aid in the debating hall at Oxford university, another centre for horrific experiments. I had spoken about some of the psychological motives underlying the mind of the vivisector who works 40 hours a week or more experimenting on helpless animals. One person in the audience said with anger and passion, 'One of the things you overlooked is that these vivisectionists are sadists.' Her comment reflected some of the outraged feelings of the extremist animal right activists. The laboratories are generally regarded (and understandably, I feel) as an animal Auschwitz or animal Belsen, as inhumane as the Nazi concentration camps.

The intensity of such work, with such little benefit to the imprisoned creatures, has its consequences. The work to transform the state of one's consciousness and the work to establish social justice appear to be such tremendous undertakings that frequently the concern for one precludes the other.

The danger is that working on one's own consciousness, it seems to me, can lead to a forgetfulness, if not blindness, to the world and its sufferings. The danger of focusing on social justice is that neglecting one's consciousness can result in burnout.

I was not altogether surprised when Jean Pink told me that she had left the animal rights movement. After some months, she became a disciple of the American guru, Master Da Free John. Some of those who are regarded as being spiritually well-informed, such as the late Alan Watts and the contemporary writer Ken Wilbur, speak of Master Da in the same breath as Jesus or Buddha. Others regard him as yet another charismatic religious figure commanding a small group of loyal devotees. Master Da, formerly Bubba Free John, has changed his name twice again, first to Master Da Love Ananda, and now Da Avadhoota. He lives on a Pacific island in Fiji with a group of followers.

Jean lives in North London in a house which she shares with six other students of the teacher. She helps The Laughing Man Institute, founded by Master Da, with administration, organizing seminars and various cultural events. Jean met Master Da when he visited Amsterdam and London in 1986.

The interview, which took place at the Laughing Man Bookshop just off Oxford Street in London, traces from the time Jean became involved in animal rights to her present involvement with the teachings of Master Da. In an honest and frank way, she recalls some of the highlights of her personal journey.

CT: How did you become involved in animal rights and the struggle against vivisection?

JP: I happened to pick up a book in a library called *Animal Liberation* by Peter Singer. I had never read a book of that sort before. I was horrified by what I learnt – about the way in which millions of animals are suffering in laboratories and factory farms. I couldn't forget it. As the days and weeks went by I began to feel that I wanted to bring about some change in that area. The book showed what was happening to animals behind closed doors in our so-called civilized society. I had always felt that people in England had some feeling for animals but when I learnt that five million experiments were done every year in which animals were blinded, scalded, traumatized, poisoned to death, and so on, I was deeply shocked. I couldn't believe this was happening. The majority are small mammals, like rats, mice and guinea pigs. Others are larger animals – primates: dogs, cats, monkeys and rabbits.

CT: So you had to do something about the situation. What was the next step?

JP: I had been conditioned to believe that we live in a democratic society and therefore I assumed there was something that I, as a citizen, could do. So I began to find out what was already being done. I wrote to all the main societies that I could find that were involved in working against such treatment of animals. I wrote to the Royal Society for the Prevention of Cruelty to Animals, the British Union for the Abolition of Vivisection and the National Anti-Vivisection Society, which were the main societies at the time against vivisection. I was not particularly impressed with the material I received from them or their campaigning methods. I felt they were very low key and they weren't bringing this matter to public notice. So it seemed that there was a gap that needed to be filled.

Well, I immediately had the thought, 'But what can I do? I am just one individual. I have no money. I have no support.' So I thought, at least I could, perhaps, organize a petition and put some pressure on the Home Office to show that some people were concerned. So I wrote a letter to several local newspapers and put some facts in the letter about the suffering experienced by animals in laboratories. I asked people to contact me if they would like to help get a petition together. As a result, seventeen or eighteen people wrote or telephoned and said that they would like to help.

I was asking for a change in the law which would give animals in the laboratories proper protection so that they didn't suffer during the experiments. I didn't think at that stage there was any point in asking the Home Office to abolish experiments. We collected about 6,000 signatures. I sent the petition and signatures to the Home Office and we received a nonsense reply. It was obvious they threw the petition straight into the waste paper basket. That was a waste of time. Most of the people weren't interested in going any further than that. I discovered that another group had started up. They were doing something which seemed to me to be much more useful. They were actually standing outside the offices of companies involved in animal experiments. They gave out leaflets and held up banners in protest. In this way, they attracted publicity and alerted the public.

I decided to join them and we went to a cosmetics company called Rimmel in Cavendish Square in London. The purpose of the demonstration was not simply to protest but to persuade the Managing Director that the company should investigate alternative methods of testing their products or at least finance research in this area. There was a doctor from our first group, Dr Whittal, who was totally offended by the animal experiments. We contacted him to find out if he wanted to join us and he did. He researched the scientific journals to find out what was happening currently in laboratories and then we put the details of these experiments on leaflets and duplicated them in my kitchen on an old hand-operated duplicator. Then we took the information in great bags up to London from Tonbridge and gave them to the public outside railway stations during the rush hour. They would read them on their way home on the train. We gradually received donations and offers of help, as well as requests for information of future demonstrations. It was very exciting. We were tapping into a need as people woke up to what was going on. By the end of the year I realized I couldn't continue with my job and do this work of running Animal Aid at the same time. I was losing interest in the job because my heart was in this.

CT: Were there other Animal Aid projects?

JP: We started a newspaper, which gave details of demonstrations, reports of activities and information on vegetarian food. Through small advertisements in nationwide journals, the organization grew and people in other parts of the country began giving out leaflets. So I found myself packing up many large parcels of leaflets. When we were finally able to have the leaflets done at the printers, we would order 10,000 leaflets at a time. Within two years we were ordering a million leaflets at a time. That's when we campaigned against Revlon cosmetics, which was first initiated by an animal rights activist, Henry Spira in New York.

CT: Why was Revlon chosen among the cosmetic companies to campaign against?

JP: Henry Spira and his friends made Revlon the target because they felt it was useless to attack the whole cosmetics industry; it could easily be shrugged off. It was better to target one leading company. In the USA, companies have to declare the number of animals they use every year for experiments. In Britain we don't have the Freedom of Information Act so the public cannot get hold of such information. He could obtain information on the exact number of rabbits used in the Draize Test in a given year by the company. He also acquired a copy of a film made for laboratory technicians, showing the method used in the test and the results on the rabbits' eyes.

Draize testing is commonly used in many countries. In order to find out how toxic a substance is in such products as hairspray, or mascara, or anything which may come into contact with the eyes, they drip the substance into the rabbit's eyes and leave it there. Each rabbit is held in a stock so that its head can't move; the animal is kept there for days. They choose rabbits because rabbits don't have tear ducts so the substance can't wash out. The substance can cause considerable damage to the cornea. The technicians assess the damage to the rabbit's eyes at various times after the drip. The film shows horrendous photographs of damaged eyes of these helpless rabbits. It is still the most commonly used test.

CT: The public argument is that we need these tests in order to protect the consumer. What is your response?

JP: I have two responses to this. One is: Do we need any more hair lacquer, mascara and all the rest of it? The second is: Can they test these products in another way than through experiments on animals? They haven't used other methods simply because this is the way it has always been done. You can use products from Beauty Without Cruelty, a cosmetic company that doesn't sell injurious products. There are many cruelty-free products available. The major companies would say to us that they are in business and have to keep producing new products every year because this is a very competitive field. We put pressure on this particular company by publicizing what they were doing in a big way and then saying to them, 'Why don't you give money to scientists to research alternatives?' We gave them that option.

CT: How big is Revlon?

JP: It is the leading cosmetic company in the States. The heading of the leaflets was, 'Revlon Tortures Rabbits'. It was printed in a big typeface. We had contacts in Australia, France, South Africa, Sweden, Switzerland and other countries. We co-ordinated a day called, 'Remember the Revlon Rabbits Day'. We organized for activists to be outside the big stores that sold Revlon products, except in South Africa where such demonstrations are not permitted. We had people outside stores selling cosmetics in almost every town and city in England. Activists dressed up as rabbits and the press, radio and television gave us tremendous publicity. We held one demonstration outside the office of the Managing Director of Revlon on Bond Street in London's West End. I remember the demonstration. It was very loud and noisy. He had telephoned me and asked me to come and see him. He said to me, 'I'm not a cruel person.' He was obviously very concerned. The demonstration took place less than four weeks before Christmas. On Christmas Eve I received a telephone call from Henry in New York to tell me that Revlon had held a press conference that morning. They announced a $1,000,000 donation to the Rockefeller Institute to research alternatives to the Draize Test.

CT: What did you do after that?

JP: The next thing was that someone in Northampton [England] heard that Avon Cosmetics, another large American-based company, was about to open a new wing in the town and that they had invited Princess Anne to come down and open it. This person in Northampton said, 'How about doing a big demonstration?' I said, 'Great.' We quickly printed some 'Avon Tortures Rabbits' leaflets identical to the Revlon leaflets, because Avon used exactly the same experiments on rabbits.

We had all the leaflets ready when I had a telephone call from Henry who said that he and his friends had decided on the second target – Avon. I told him that we had beaten him to it. He advised me to send some leaflets to the Managing Director and request that Avon should donate $1,000,000 like Revlon. After I sent the leaflets, I had a long telex back the next day from the Managing Director inviting me to go to Northampton to see him and discuss the issue. I rang him and said I was sorry I couldn't come because I was too busy working on the 'Avon Tortures Rabbits' campaign!

CT: What did he do?

JP: Well, he came down in his chauffeur-driven car. He again told the story that they didn't want to have to do these animal experiments, but how could they possibly do anything else? What else could they do to protect their consumers? I told him it was shameful. A few weeks went by and then Avon donated $750,000 to research.

It then became difficult to find large enough companies to target who were not also involved in drugs used in the medical field. With drugs you enter into a completely different field. You are not talking simple issues then. Cosmetics are not something that you have to have and also there are alternatives like cruelty-free cosmetics. But when you get into drugs, you are talking about life and death. That's another story altogether.

When we looked into the experiments that were being performed on animals in the universities allegedly for medical research, more often than not they were being done for cold curiosity.

CT: Again the public's rationalization for experiments for medicine is that it is absolutely necessary to protect human life. In many people's eyes, human life has much more value than an animal's life.

JP: Yes, that's true but we wanted to show people that much sickness was preventable. So we began to promote alternative medicine as well as healthy living and a healthy diet. We wanted to be positive. These tests on animals still go on. The Cruelty to Animals Act was passed in 1876. We worked very hard for seven years and the sum total of our success is very small indeed. We got a lot of public support. There is certainly a lot more awareness of what is going on. In 1985 there was a new act in Britain relating to laboratory animals, but it did almost nothing to improve the lot of the animals. It's a useless act. I began to lose my interest at that point.

One of the curious factors was that we had great difficulty in dealing with a very militant fringe in the animal rights movement. These people actually wanted to go out and kill vivisectors. They were violent and very angry and believed in the use of violent methods. We were battling with them almost as much as we were battling with the companies and the scientists. That didn't make me leave, but it did undermine my enthusiasm to some degree. There were some people in the movement who sanctioned violence and who spent a lot of time criticizing people who were into peaceful demonstrations. So we found ourselves engaged in ridiculous scuffles with these people and it was very frustrating. The fanatics would come and ruin our marches. The last march I was involved in organizing for Animal Aid took place in Bristol. The police and the press were there and on the television news that night, it looked as if Animal Aid was a violent society.

I began to move away from the mainstream of animal rights, and with a group of people started up an organization called Campaign for Healthy Food. We wanted to show that to avoid sickness was better than to get sick and rely on animal experiments. But it was almost a desperate move on my part. I did not have a great feeling that this would succeed. It didn't. Healthy food does not grab people. People were not going to give us money to support that. But if you show pictures of animals that are suffering terribly, then people are motivated to respond.

CT: Since the healthy food campaign never really got underway, where did it leave you?

JP: It left me in a vacuum. I wasn't clear what I was going to do at all. I felt like a rudderless ship. Some months later I happened to pick up a copy of *Resurgence* magazine with an intriguing review of two books by Master Da Free John. I went to The Laughing Man Institute here in London and found out they were showing videos of Master Da Free John. I was very moved by what I saw and impressed by the people at the Institute. I signed up for a seven-week course which was an introduction to Da Free's teaching and his life. I knew right away without a doubt that I had found my teacher and I have had no doubts at all in three years.

When I saw the videos I felt a strong response. I can't explain it at all. I just knew in my heart that he was who he said he was. There was a strange sensation between my eyebrows, an electrical feeling or vibration and when I left the bookshop to catch the train it was as if I was walking on air. It was incredible.

CT: What do you mean when you say that you knew Da Free John was who he said he was?

JP: He proclaims that he is what we are already. He has realized it and we haven't. In other words, he is the divine being incarnate, which is the same as us. But we are obstructed because of the 'egoic' activities going on in our mind, in the conceptional mind, that we can't be what we already are. But he quite clearly, to me, was that. He was so free. Incredible freedom. It shows.

CT: How does it show?

JP: In his body and mind. In his gestures. It is just obvious to see it. You can intuit that freedom by seeing him and hearing him. You can intuit a person by being with him.

CT: But you actually hadn't met him.

JP: No. I find that in reading certain parts of his books there is something physical that occurs. It was the same as when I saw the video. That particular video had a dramatic effect. Yes. It is a bit like falling in love but much more profound. It is not a cultic attachment. He criticizes that very strongly indeed. In a cultic attachment you want something back from the person. It is a childish relationship. That does not bring about maturity as a human being. It is a very immature situation to be looking up to this great guru and to be enthusiastically proclaiming his great virtues. That is not what his teaching is about. He constantly undermines that because there is always that tendency in us.

CT: If that is a childish relationship to such a human being then what is an adult relationship?

JP: An adult relationship to a spiritual teacher exists when the student or disciple is willing to take on the spiritual practice that he offers, and the great discipline that is required in that practice. The teacher points out that living in this world is not about seeking for some form of self-fulfilment. The true purpose of life is self-transcendence in every moment of the day based on self-observation in the context of daily life and the understanding that comes out of this. It becomes obvious to the practitioner that the ego is always seeking self-fulfilment of one sort or another. So there is a constant demand to be attentive to one's patterns of seeking. Such an activity requires a certain maturity and has nothing to do with child-like devotion. He makes one realize that it is possible to be that free, but he constantly brings a demand for practice in this relationship so that there is always this confrontation with the ego. There is a great deal of *sadhana* [spiritual work] involved and it takes many years in most cases.

CT: Isn't there the danger of using Master Da as a model of what it is to be free? In this case, the belief is that one becomes free through contact with the persona of Master Da Free John.

JP: He criticizes very strongly any form of idealism. We have all fallen into this trap a lot. He has shown very clearly that this is not what the way is about – realizing some ideal by copying him or somebody else. It is not about that at all. It is about simply being aware of the tendency, on the one hand, towards idealism and on the other hand, towards self-indulgence. We can see them both as two sides of the same coin – seeing without any form of judgement. Master Da Free John says stand in the prior position, which is already there. It's only because we get bound up in one or other of the two that we find ourselves in a dilemma. It is a matter of standing free of that and observing what is going on in the moment without being caught up in it. So it is not a question of trying to be like him, though we would like to be free, of course.

CT: I still wonder why it is important to have the additional factor of the teacher figure having a special place in the whole scheme of things.

JP: It would not be possible for me to engage in this very difficult practice, which brings happiness as well as difficulty, without that relationship. Because of his enlightened condition, he is a transmitter of a spiritual force. When one's practice is sufficiently mature then one is in a position to receive this spiritual power and that practice is a form of purification. As one matures more in one's practice, then one doesn't look upon him as the teacher any more but as the divine. There is a different relationship then between the devotee and the guru than there is at this stage which I am at in which I relate to him as a teacher. Without him there is no transmission. Not in that direct sense.

CT: Isn't the divine or transcendent to be perceived everywhere with everyone in a direct way rather than isolating one particular human being from the great mass of humanity?

JP: He says that everything is God. There is nothing else but God. But most people that one meets don't actually demonstrate that. They demonstrate basically a certain contraction from that.

CT: Have you let go of political and social activism for a commitment with a spiritual master?

JP: I let go of the commitment to campaign for social or political change for many months before I came across Master Da Free John. I had already lost interest in campaigning.

CT: Is there any connection or relationship between the ending of activism and this relationship with the teacher?

JP: I don't see any relationship between these two parts of my life. You see, basically for the past 25 years or more I have been interested in some form of spiritual life. It has been a very long and varied adventure in seeking into different areas, like Krishnamurti, Jung, Tibetan Buddhism, as well as insight meditation retreats with you. So spirituality has been an underlying theme in my life. The seven years in animal rights was something different. But it was just a seven-year period which began and finished and that was it. This involvement in the present teaching is much more to do with my whole orientation to life.

CT: Can you envisage an approach which sustains your day-to-day commitment to these spiritual teachings and to social–political work at the same time? Can you foresee a marriage between these two?

JP: If a person does actually transcend themselves in their ordinary day-to-day activities they obviously will change and that person will become a different person from the one they were before. Therefore, that in itself effects change without being involved in any goal of change. The mere existence of a person of that maturity must bring about change in and of itself. That is what Master Da is teaching. His aim is to have a spiritual community on this planet before he dies, with people who can be agents of this change, of this way that he is teaching. At the moment it seems like it is rather far off because basically he says, 'We do not want the heat of *sadhana* [spiritual work] on our backs.' He says we are really ambiguous in our commitment because we are constantly looking around the corner at some other thing that we want to do. A community of realized people can have an amazing effect on this planet, greater than anything else.

CT: You are saying, first and foremost is the necessity for self-transcendence.

JP: Yes. For example, discipline is not just a hard grind. These people are into a very committed disciplined life and they are happy. It is not like puritanical religion. That is something we can all respond to.

CT: Can the Earth wait for this ideal to find its actual manifestation on the planet? The Earth is already in crisis. Don't we need to be working on ourselves and for the planet simultaneously? Doesn't it take enormous faith to accept the view that self-transcendence will come first and then, afterwards, this self-transcendence will generate an impact all over the Earth?

JP: We are in the world. We are not sitting in monasteries. Master Da says that we must have jobs and not hide ourselves away from the community. We are already involved. I am involved in teaching but there is very little that I can do to put across my ideas because the real way I would like to be teaching is impossible. The education set-up is such that they can't accommodate what I would want. I am teaching deeply disturbed children or children with extreme learning difficulties individually. I can't commit myself to class teaching in the state system. Also children today are so wild. You need a strong physical constitution and a loud voice. I can't do it.

It need not take long for a realized community to come about in the world. It could be ten years or twenty years. Think how long we have waited for change on this planet. By engaging in campaigns and so on there has been some change. Basically, we are still in a very bad situation despite all the idealistic campaigning going on, including nuclear disarmament, animal rights, women's rights and all that stuff. In the midst of such work many of us were constantly frustrated by our own egoic tendencies. We would screw up the whole work. We were basically not conscious of what was going on underneath.

I can give you a personal example. I was so one-pointed about animal rights I realized I handled the people working with me in the office in an unconscious way. I realized later that I was very unfeeling towards them. I was out of touch because I had this one idea in mind, one goal. If they didn't fit in exactly with what I wanted, I tended to dramatize my frustration. That's what happens all the time in life when people are unaware of themselves, or don't understand their own motivation.

CT: Psychotherapy, spirituality and communication skills are contributing to integration with social–political work. Among those connected with Master Da, are there any who actively express a political social awareness?

JP: When people first become involved they are asked to study Master Da Free John's teaching together with a number of selected texts from The Great Tradition of spiritual life, i.e. Buddhism, Hinduism, Christianity and others. Students are encouraged to study these works with seriousness and discrimination. They then begin to apply the Teaching in their lives and at some point, depending on the response of the individual student, they take on disciplines relating to all areas of their lives, i.e. diet, service, exercise, sex, work, which serve as a self-reflecting mechanism. The student begins to see the patterns of his/her particular forms of seeking for consolation and so the process of self-observation becomes more and more profound. As far as I know there is no direct involvement by practitioners in any form of campaigning work, but many of them are sympathetic to the various causes.

We are all to blame

An interview with John Seed
Sydney, Australia

> *'I am protecting the rainforest'*
> *develops into*
> *'I am part of the rainforest protecting myself'*
> *develops into*
> *'I am that part of that rainforest*
> *recently emerged into thinking.'*

The above words of John Seed, the founder/director of the Rainforest Information Centre in Lismore, New South Wales, Australia, have been widely quoted around the world by ecologists and environmental activists at many conferences and public lectures.

Since 1979 he has been fully involved in the protection of rainforests, especially tropical rainforests, throughout the world. He is a firm advocate of deep ecology – a movement which shows the necessity for human beings to undergo a profound change in consciousness towards living on the earth. He says that when people see through the layers of anthropocentric (i.e. human chauvinist, self-cherishing) ways of living, a most profound change in the perception of life begins to take place.

John employs a fourfold emphasis in communicating the ongoing crisis of the rainforests, in which every year eleven million acres are destroyed simply for the sake of human convenience. First, he stresses the importance of increasing public knowledge of the plight of the rainforests through newsletters, articles and leaflets. Second, he supports active participation in non-violent protest either in the forests themselves or at offices of the industries responsible for the destruction of the forests, as well as the boycott of goods. Third, he engages in active dialogue with the businesses and governments involved. Fourth, he holds public meetings and workshops that employ teaching and communication aids, meditations, spiritual exercises and rituals.

In 1986, he co-produced with Jeni Kendell, *Earth First*, an hour-long documentary on the history of the struggle for the Australian rainforests, a film available on video from their Lismore office.

In 1987, John organized and led the first Australian, 'Earth First! Rainforest Roadshow'. The roadshow gave 20 gigs in 20 nights along 1500 miles of the East Coast of Australia. There were also three 'Councils of All Beings' workshops and rituals to awaken people's hearts, minds and bodies to their roots in the tropical rainforests tens of thousands of years ago. In the meditations and exercises, groups experience their ecological being as life elements in common with all other forms of life elements. People share songs, poems and other experiences, moving toward feeling themselves as 'leaves on the tree of life'. The roadshow raised some £4,000 for rainforest activists in Ecuador and the Solomon Islands.

Prior to 1979 John was a student of Buddhism and insight meditation. He participated in a number of retreats in Dalhousie in the foothills of the Himalayas during the mid-1970s. Upon his return to Australia he moved to what is known as the 'Rainbow Region' of Australia, the northern part of New South Wales. There was a migration of so-called hippies to this area, since land was cheap and available. Numerous small communities were started up.

John helped found the Forest Meditation Centre and Bodhi Farm, a 160-acre piece of land at The Channon, near Lismore. Bodhi Farm has gained widespread publicity in Australia in recent years for the various successful campaigns it has engaged in with regard to rights of small communities.

Currently, he is the editor of the *World Rainforest Report* and has helped establish rainforest action groups in Australia, USA, Japan, Europe and in Third World countries where most of the rainforests are found.

The interview with John was held one morning in Sydney while travelling by car to the airport through the morning traffic. I was on my way to the Rainbow region of northern New South Wales and John was holding evening meetings with city-based activists.

CT: Why do you feel that it is important to preserve the rainforest?

JS: I think it is essential to protect the earth's eco-system and because the rainforests are the most dense collection of genetic material and species in the world, with over half the world's 10 million species of plants and animals living there. It's not really more essential to preserve the rainforests than to preserve species generally. The rainforests are a symbol for all species, a symbol for genetic diversity.

There is also the non-anthropocentric reason. The rainforests are worth preserving because they exist and they have the right to exist and for no other reason than that. This is reason enough for their continued existence. We appeal to people to consider that these species have as long and illustrious a history as our own species, having all evolved from a common ancestor about four and a half billion years ago. We have no right to terminate other species.

Another reason is within a human frame of reference. Here too there are many reasons not to exterminate species. Every species is part of the same web of life of which we are a part. There is no separation between us and the rest of nature. To damage nature is to damage ourselves. To think we can damage nature without doing harm to ourselves is to misunderstand who we are.

CT: How would we damage ourselves?

JS: There would be a spiritual damage. There would also be a direct material damage to ourselves because the food, building materials, industrial products and medicines that we depend on don't exist in isolation from the rest of nature. As we wipe out our wild genetic ancestors then we wipe out food and medicine that the rainforests provide for us now and in the future.

For example, when a new disease comes along to blight one of our crops, the only way that we can preserve that crop is by going out into the wilderness to find the wild ancestors of that crop to look for traits which are able to meet that new threat, whatever it is. Crops and vegetables are highly vulnerable to any kind of change in climate and to other environmental changes. They are also vulnerable to the parasites and predators that are evolving. Our crops have to keep evolving in order to continue to exist. Large stocks of wild genetic material need to keep evolving. We can't duplicate life in the laboratories.

CT: We use the resources of the rainforests. What is the present degree of damage or destruction to the rainforests and what areas on the earth are most seriously affected?

JS: There is some controversy about the degree of destruction. Projections based on satellite photographs show that within the next thirty years, all remaining accessible areas of rainforest will have been damaged or destroyed. There is no forest anywhere not being destroyed at an immense rate, especially in Central America, South America, Africa, South East Asia and the Pacific, where most of the rainforests exist.

CT: Who is destroying these forests?

JS: We all are – due to the products that we consume and the lifestyle that we lead. There are two basic problems. On the one hand, there is the standard of living and rate of consumption in the so-called developed world, where masses of people are living in a luxury that no king or emperor could have dreamed of a couple of centuries ago. Basically people are consuming the future. We *could* consume in a sustainable way. We could consume the increment of what nature produces without consuming the capital. The capital is the species and the non-renewable resources. We *could* imagine ourselves continuing to evolve for hundreds and thousands or millions of years into the future. At present we are consuming those thousands and millions of years within a few generations. Within this time, we will have consumed all of our 'future'.

   On the other hand, there's the question of the growing population in the so-called 'under-developed world', where huge areas of forests are being destroyed by slash and burn agriculture to meet the needs of the rising population and rising material aspirations as well. No room is left for wild nature to continue.

CT: To protect the rainforests, there has to be a real change in our attitude in the West and elsewhere to our relationship with material wealth. A brake also has to be placed on population growth. As individuals, how can we work with these major global issues?

JS: My whole life is spent trying to answer that question. I would suggest that a fundamental change in consciousness right through the human species is necessary. For instance, for 51 per cent of the human species to make the change wouldn't be sufficient. Basically an evolution of the collective understanding of all people is the only basis for a resolution of this situation. Reforms are useless. There are no other measures that are going to be of any use at this point because the rate of destruction is so fast and the momentum of the whole human enterprise is so immense that there can be no temporary victories, such as declaring a particular rainforest as a national park. None of those things are of any real use.

CT: So the change cannot be made just by legislation. There has to be a change in the consciousness of human beings towards an awareness of their relationship to the earth. In Judaism and Christianity, that emphasis isn't so much present. How can a Christian look at this new way in the light of his or her Christian beliefs?

JS: There is a very interesting paper written on this subject called 'The Historical Basis for the Environmental Crisis', by Lynn White Jr., an American professor of history. In this paper he lays the blame down squarely on the doorstep of Judeo-Christian basic creation myths, which say that the planet was created for the benefit of human beings. 'They will be in fear and trembling of us' and all the rest of what is found in the Bible.

CT: In Genesis it says, 'Man shall have dominion over the earth.'

JS: This is the kind of problem we are faced with. It is not so much that everybody still believes this, though many still do, but rather the whole basis for our culture is inextricably corrupted by such unecological beliefs. There are Christians, particularly the fundamentalist Christians in America, who believe in the literal truth of the Bible. I would say that this belief system is among the most dangerous that exist on earth.

A prime example was James Watt, who was the Environment Secretary in the Reagan administration. When he was asked whether we should not be saving some of these non-renewable resources for future generations he expressed his opinion that there were not going to be many future generations before the coming of the Lord. Watt said it was really our duty to use up the bounty that had been given to us. He seemed to be saying that there was some morality dictating us to continue to use up these resources!

CT: I attended an eco-theology seminar in Totnes. One of the participating American professors, who was a Christian, said the basic relationship of the creator with the creation is that human beings are, in fact, co-creators with God. Our responsibility is to develop a caring and sensitive awareness of our relationship to the earth.

JS: I feel that is an important step but nevertheless we need to go further than that. That perception still contains the same sort of basic humanistic arrogance of the human species. It is similar to the notion that we will now be co-pilots of spaceship Earth. It means there is nature and there are human beings who have the right to direct and control nature. Such beliefs fill some people with great pride, whereas it fills me with immense horror. We have already damaged the earth. Having destroyed the natural life-support systems, we may have to construct replacements. Soon, perhaps, we will have no choice but to be co-pilots of the earth where we will have to create the oxygen, create the clean water, create the cycles that bring us nutrients and break down the waste.

CT: How can we look at our relationship to the earth and to nature and the materials of the earth in a balanced way?

JS: I think there are a number of answers to the question 'how'. First we can internalize the understandings of ecology and biology in the same way that we have internalized these other strange creation myths. I don't think that there are many people who really believe in the idea that an elderly gentleman with a white beard created the world in the year 4600 BC. But so many actions are based on that kind of outlook.

How do we internalize insights about the earth? Well, meditation is one useful approach. For myself I have found that direct action in defence of nature has had the strongest influence on me because in demonstrating to others and to the media, I was also demonstrating to myself a certain kind of commitment. I felt a great change took place in me as a result of placing myself in a stressful situation where I was in danger – in danger of being arrested, of being branded a criminal and of being judged.

CT: Both meditative processes and direct action express one's commitment to the earth. How did the Rainforest Information Centre come about?

JS: I was living at Bodhi Farm, a meditation community at Terana Creek in northern New South Wales. A rainforest conflict developed in our watershed only five or six miles from where we were living. I can't recall why we went to see what was happening but most of my community went and we were profoundly influenced by what went on in the next few weeks. We engaged in direct confrontation with the Forestry Commission of the state of New South Wales to try to stop the logging. We non-violently blockaded their equipment; we camped there for a month and hundreds of people were arrested. That was in 1979. Some people climbed up into the trees that had been marked for felling. They put their lives in danger in order to demonstrate ostensibly to others, and most importantly to themselves, the degree of commitment they felt for the life processes and what was threatened there. One friend of mine spent six days up in a tree hanging in a kind of fishnet. As the bulldozers went past, they'd strike the tree. His life was certainly in danger.

CT: Were these direct actions successful?

JS: In the first instance it was successful. A temporary halt was called to the logging and an inquiry took place. The inquiry didn't come up with a result that suited us, though. It was sort of rigged by the person who was conducting the inquiry who was chosen by our opponent, the Commissioner of Forests. We abandoned the inquiry before it came to its conclusions and we went back to direct action in the same mountain range, Mount Nardi, a few miles further up. That was in 1981. We spent four months camped upon the mountain. Then an opinion poll was conducted after months and months of headlines and television news. It seemed that we had successfully got our views across to the people of New South Wales. An opinion poll conducted by the National Trust found that about 70 per cent of the people wanted an end to rainforest logging and then the government legislated. So the area we were protecting passed from forestry to National Park. Six or seven other areas were declared National Park in New South Wales at that time as well.

CT: Few people, however, live anywhere near a rainforest. Even fewer people have ever stepped inside one. People do not have any sense of the awesome beauty of the tropical rainforest.

JS: I think it would be a good idea to try to spend some time in a rainforest, particularly in a meditative state of mind. What I like to do is to lie down in a rainforest when it is dry enough and cover myself in leaves and twigs and try to remember my own history. From such a forest, less than five million years ago, my ancestors emerged. I try to allow a re-connection with the immense intelligence that exists in that sort of forest. It gives rise to my intelligence and five million other kinds of intelligence as well.

CT: When you go into a rainforest and cover yourself with leaves, what kind of feelings do you experience?

JS: At the time I don't really experience much at all. Afterwards, when I come out of the rainforest and take stock of my life and what I am doing with it, I feel very clear. I don't get distracted easily from the work I have to do to communicate my concerns in trying to protect the rainforests and other natural systems around the world. There is a Dr. Suess children's story called *The Lorax*. It's about a creature that pops out of the stump of a tree that has been cut down. The lorax says, 'I speak for the trees as the trees have no tongues. I'm telling you, sir, at the top of my lungs? . . .'

I was in the Solomon Islands campaigning to save the rainforests there. All of the people in the Solomon Islands are Christians of one denomination or another so it was necessary to try to find a Christian context in which to explain the work that I was doing. So I said that in the Bible we are told that God created the world in five days and it was on the sixth day that he created humans. The first five days were spent creating all of these marvels and humans were created on the sixth day after the rest. If we destroy what God spent five days creating then surely this shows an immense disrespect to God. I don't know if that communicated to the people.

Another way is to see the rainforests as the ark within which the creatures continue to exist. The logging which takes place can be compared to pulling the planks from the ark to use for timber, an inappropriate use of the materials. Only in the ark can the animals and birds continue to survive on earth.

CT: In other words by touching people's deep religious beliefs you hope to affect their perceptions of their environment. Why did you choose to go to the Solomon Islands?

JS: It was the result of an invitation I received at a victory party to celebrate the stopping of the logging on the Nightcap Range and other rainforests in New South Wales. I met a man from the Solomon Islands. He had come to Australia in search of help to protect the rainforests in his country. The work for the rainforests in New South Wales had just ended after three years campaigning, so I was available at the time. I found that the large multi-nationals were basically scalping these most beautiful islands from one end to the other.

CT: Can you name any of these companies?

JS: Unilever is an English–Dutch company. They are the largest trading multi-national in the world with an annual turnover of one billion dollars, which is about 300 times the size of the Solomon Islands economy.

CT: In light of what you saw, would you recommend boycotting their products?

JS: Actually they have changed. Since our encounter with them they have become a rather exemplary logging company in the Solomon Islands. They fired their general manager and changed their methods of logging, from total clear felling, no protection of stream banks, no ecological sensitivity whatsoever, to standards of logging which would compare with the kind of standards we are used to in a country like Australia.

CT: Is this good propaganda and publicity put out by Unilever or have you actually witnessed the change?

JS: We have witnessed the change. The forest department in the Solomon Islands have said, 'Please don't attack Unilever. They are an example to the rest of the logging companies in the Solomons.'

CT: What brought about Unilever's change in attitude?

JS: The people in the Solomon Islands think it's because we threatened to publicize what they were doing, which would have caused an international boycott of their products. But, of course, the Unilever people never actually said that to us.

CT: Well, they wouldn't, of course. What about the large Japanese interests which seem determined to protect their forests in Japan and go overseas for their wood?

JS: Over 70 per cent of Japan is forested and most of that forest is protected. But I believe that the protection is temporary. They realize that they can get wood more cheaply in South East Asia and in the Pacific than in Japan itself. This leaves the wood in Japan available for some future time. Some people in Japan feel that their own forests are sacred. The point is, though, that the Japanese purchase nearly all of the timber that is logged on the islands. It may be Unilever that is logging but the logs are then taken to Japan.

CT: Are there other multi-nationals whose record isn't examplary?

JS: In the Solomon Islands, the companies are mostly from Korea and Taiwan. It is pretty hard to get any kind of handle on them in the way you can with Unilever. In Brazil, for example, the largest single cattle ranching operation is owned by Volkswagen. In order to clear an area of the Amazon for cattle they lit the biggest forest fire that has ever existed. They cleared thousands and thousands of square miles. Multi-nationals are diversifying into all kinds of different businesses. The nature of multi-national corporations is to go after profit. That is their only criterion. A profit can be made in cattle ranching; the beef market is expanding so Volkswagen got involved.

CT: What can one do to bring this to the notice of the general public?

JS: I contacted the German green groups with the idea of producing bumper stickers to put on other people's cars, rather than one's own car, to put out information about what Volkswagen is doing. Hopefully this would decrease the sales of their cars and bring about a change in the company's attitude toward the rainforests. These actions are to create a public awareness.

One of the questions which you asked me was how the necessary sort of change in awareness could take place. That is something which I have been really feeling frustrated with, both the direct action and these kinds of actions with Volkswagen because at times such actions seem peripheral to the actual issue.

It actually reminds me of the story of Mulla Nasruddin, the Sufi sage, searching for his key under the lamp rather than where he had lost it. I feel the solution is out in the dark, but I'm searching under the street lamp because at least there is some light there. So I've started taking some steps into the dark. One step is into exploring new rituals. We have been performing them by taking time on solstices and equinoxes to do rituals to reaffirm the depth of commitment and connection we feel with the earth.

CT: Ritual is a tremendous vehicle. It seems to me in my travels around the world that there is a whole area here for exploration.

JS: I went to a workshop on Despair and Empowerment with Dr Joanna Macy. The central despair ritual in that workshop involved people calling out the kind of things that they saw happening in the world that led to despair and then other people would call out 'I hear you. I hear you.' Anyone who felt like weeping would go to a certain place and weep. People who were angry would beat pillows. Despair, anger, sadness gripped the whole room. It was a very moving experience which led to feelings of greater commitment and empowerment. During the feedback session at the end of the workshop, part of my criticism of the process was that 10 million species are in danger, yet most of the people were calling out and reflecting on issues that were human-centred issues like famine, poverty and abuse of children. Only a few were despairing about what was happening to animals, creatures, trees and the earth, itself.

Joanna came back to Bodhi Farm and we talked about constructing a non-anthropocentric despair ritual. We decided to call it the 'Council of All Beings'. Before the despair ritual we identify with an animal, plant or some feature of the landscape. Then we make masks to represent our ally, or totem. During the ritual we wear the masks; we represent the myriad species and we call out on their behalf. Participants have a very positive experience and both Joanna and I have had a number of these rituals since then.

CT: Concerned women are encouraging all of us to be aware of the intuitive, caring and loving factors we feel towards the welfare of the ecosystem. One of the bridges which is being examined is a re-examination of the value of paganism. Through ritual and ceremony, we pay full respect and give full acknowledgement to nature. This fits in with what you are saying.

JS: I'm really interested in this process. From the 'Council of All Beings' ritual, we also took another step which was a development of rebirthing therapy, which we call 'Breath'. In rebirthing, people use a connected breathing technique developed by Stan Grof to move into deeper layers of their own being to resolve personal problems. People are often moved to tears or anger through this therapy and also have profound insights about themselves and life. The 'Breath' process adds another element to rebirthing, which is intention. Before each person begins they decide on an intention for what they will work on during the session. Then they discuss this with the group leaders. It does seem that the experience one has during such a session is often related to the intention that one takes into the session.

We then began adding non-personal intentions, which developed into another ritual called 'Eco-breath'. Given that there is in reality no separation between person and planet, that any sense of alienation or isolation is illusory, we may use this breathing technique to tap into transpersonal, and even trans-species awareness. This became a four-day workshop. People find a partner and each one takes it in turn to lie down and breathe, and the other cares for the breather. The kind of intentions that we used were: 'I intend to experience through my sadness the message from the rainforests and their response to our separation from them.' Another intention was: 'I intend to look at the way to heal and restore the antagonisms between women and men on the planet.' So people's intentions were both personal and planetary.

CT: So here was a therapy working together with global awareness.

JS: Yes. These rituals have become a way of our tapping into the planet, to the creatures, the trees and life forms. In this way the experience of the person is not separate from the rest of the planet. Through experiencing our own pain we may be tapping into the planet's pain and through healing ourselves we may thus contribute to the healing of the earth.

CT: So through new rituals you are stepping out of the familiar expressions of concern to explore fresh ways for all of us to get in touch with ourselves and work to heal both ourselves and the planet. Are you feeling any disappointment with direct action?

JS: Direct action is good but it isn't enough. The only justification I can see for it is to change people's minds. We might be able to damage Volkswagen's reputation so that they are forced to stop cattle ranching in the Amazon and so protest does increase public awareness of the problem, but all it does is replace one cattle ranch company in the Amazon with another. Volkswagen will sell their interests and someone else will buy them. As far as the Amazon is concerned, nothing has changed, although people's awareness may have changed through that process.

CT: Are you saying there is no possibility of stopping the destruction of the Amazon?

JS: I'm saying there is no possibility other than through a tremendous change in people's understanding. There is no possibility of changing it by physically preventing something from taking place. None that I can see. Even if you can save this bit or that bit, the destruction that is taking place at the same time everywhere else is such that it is a little bit like tides coming in. You build a little wall on a certain patch of the beach and think you can keep the water out. But sooner or later the wall is going to go.

CT: Given your commitment to the rainforests, doesn't that leave you in a state of continual despair, frustration and disappointment?

JS: No. It leads me to look for some direct ways to change the awareness of people rather than through this indirect way of – 'Let's harass Volkswagen'. We can explore fresh ways. There is no separation between myself and anybody else. It may be that the right person thinking the right thought is heard at a distance of a 1000 miles. If we can get a clear enough shared intention then we can affect things beyond ourselves. The week after the first 'Council of All Beings' workshop some whales were stranded on the coast nearby and people went to help rescue them. The local newspaper, *The Northern Star*, which is very conservative politically, had an editorial which was headlined 'Compassion for All Beings.' Such a headline is totally out of character with *The Northern Star*. We couldn't help but wonder if the vibration around the place had changed and whether our work in the forest the previous weekend had somehow changed something.

CT: Are you saying that if *The Northern Star* can publish that sort of editorial, then there is hope?

JS: Yes, I think so. Again I'm not at all certain that this kind of approach will work but I feel desperate enough to try anything. I do feel that in the end people must understand that their self-interest cannot possibly be any different from the interests of the planet as a whole. Then we can find a way through this situation. People's sense of self has to expand beyond the shrunken social fiction of a self that we have inherited. It has to expand to a perception which really and truly believes in a shared biology.

CT: Throughout this meeting we are connecting and re-connecting with an awareness that does not separate person from planet.

Hopefully these connections can be made again and again. Thank you.

SOCIAL ACTION

We used hammers

An interview with Jim Perkins
Barre, Massachusetts, U.S.A.

'*And they shall beat their swords into plowshares,*
and their spears into pruning hooks;
Nation shall not lift up sword against nation,
Neither shall they learn war anymore.'
ISAIAH 2:4

One of the features of the peace movement that can be observed
again and again is that there are phases of massive public outpour-
ings of concern. Some of the peace demonstrations in the 1980s in
the Western world were among the largest demonstrations ever
witnessed in the history of humanity. People turned out by the
hundreds of thousands to put pressure on the superpowers to
disarm. And although the men in Washington and Moscow are
desperate to take credit for any disarmament treaties, it is really
the voice of the people that has moved them to the negotiating
table, as much as economic and political realities.

The movement for peace and justice certainly has its ebb and
flow in terms of public interest. Membership and activity tend to
be influenced by the degree of publicity an event gets. What is often
forgotten is that the issues facing people and planet do not go away.
This means that a small core of activists keep the flame of protest
alive during the weeks, months and sometimes years when the
media perceives that there is nothing newsworthy going on in the
peace movement.

One of those who keeps the flame of protest alive is Jim Perkins.
I first met Jim in 1978 when he came to participate in a retreat in

New England. He gave me an enormous jar of pure maple syrup to bring back to old England.

Jim was born in 1938. From 1961 to 1968 he taught social studies in high school and participated in the civil rights struggle as a Freedom School Teacher in Mississippi. In 1968 he founded and directed the Manhattan Country School Farm, which offered family farming and environmental skills and values to inner city children.

Jim has participated in recent years in a number of insight meditation retreats in Barre, Massachusetts. He also spent six months practising prayer and meditation at the Doshingi Monastery, Mount Tremper, New York before becoming part of a war resistance community in Maryland.

As so often happens, a meeting with someone can touch that deep place within which brings out another level of commitment to disarmament. In Jim's case, it was spending a weekend retreat with Dan Berrigan, one of the two Berrigan brothers, who were investigated by the FBI, put on trial and imprisoned for their anti-war activities. As Jim said in the interview, 'He made it very clear to me that I couldn't play around.'

Jim's newly awakened commitment to direct action led to a three-year jail sentence due to his involvement with an incident at a nuclear weapons base.

Although he is not a Christian, Jim has taken to heart the Biblical prophecy of 'they shall beat their swords into plowshares'. At the time of this writing, more than 70 people have participated in 24 Plowshare actions, which involve breaking into nuclear weapons bases and deliberately disarming parts of the weapons with hammers and pouring blood on them.

The judiciary has come down heavily on these peace activists. Sentences have ranged from six months up to staggering twelve- and eighteen-year sentences for what is basically the destruction of government property and criminal trespass. The media have paid very little attention to these actions, even when one of the cases involved a mother who was sentenced to eighteen years for her non-violent direct action.

Despite the imposition of severe sentences, peace activists with religious convictions keep coming forward to engage in such disarmament actions. As one sympathiser pointed out, 'It reveals the lengths that the government is willing to go to prosecute and jail

non-violent people who resist nuclear war and interventionist policies. It is ironic that those responsible for crimes in the Iran–Contra
[arms dealing] affair receive immunity while peace activists receive
long imprisonment for having acted in obedience to their understanding of divine and international law.'

Jim presently lives in western Massachusetts and is on parole
from the Federal Prison System, where he served 18 months of his
prison sentence before receiving parole. As a member of the national
council of FOR, the renowned religious organization for peace and
social justice, he continues his anti-war work. He is currently a
contractor and carpenter and has five children.

The interview took place during a Buddhist retreat half-way
through Jim's prison term, Jim having been granted religious fur-
lough for the weekend in order to participate. Jim kindly agreed to
have the interview in the hall and allow the other participants to
listen in while he talked about his action at the nuclear weapon
base.

JP: I want to start with some words of appreciation. It's not at
all like prison here [at the Insight Meditation Society]. In prison,
there is a background of grumbling and complaining. The food
isn't anything like it is in prison. Here at IMS, it's coming into a
classic period. I've never tasted anything like it. It's wonderful to
be with you. I wish I could be here longer.

CT: Jim, this afternoon, I would like to discuss your personal
involvement in the peace movement and I'd like to begin with the
break-in of the nuclear weapon base in Orlando, Florida in
December 1983. What were the events that led up to this period
when you and other men and women first committed yourselves to
this peace action?

JP: In December 1983, NATO began to deploy Pershing II missiles
in Europe. That was an evident shift in what the United States said
it was doing; a shift from a nuclear policy of deterrence to one of
first strike. That is attack theory. These are attack weapons and it
seemed to me important to point that out to the public and not let
that go by as a secret.

CT: What steps did you take personally? Who did you get in
contact with?

JP: I had been involved in various kinds of social action since the

early 1960s. I was campaigning for civil rights and I was involved
in the anti-Vietnam War movement. I never did anything that got
me into prison. This road to prison really started with a retreat
that I went to with Daniel Berrigan. It became very clear to me
that to be with Daniel meant I couldn't play around. I walked out
of the retreat centre onto the highway not knowing whether I was
going to go this way or that way. It was that disorientating. What
I finally did was, I went this-a-way – to live in the community
where Daniel Berrigan's brother was living. It's in Baltimore [Mary-
land], called Jonah House.

CT: For several years you have been coming here to IMS, practising Buddhist meditation. How did you fit into a Christian community and the peace work there?

JP: I fit in very well and felt very comfortable with them. In fact,
I thought that I was really seeing Christianity for the first time.
They seemed to be very comfortable with me, some more than
others. The more I kept my mouth closed, the more comfortable it
was. When I went to Jonah House I already pretty much knew
what I was getting into; that was part of the decision. Both Philip
and Daniel Berrigan were part of the first Plowshares action in
1980. They have been a guiding force in this movement since that
time.

CT: So you went to the base four months later. What took place
in the period between December 1983 and Easter Sunday, when
you entered the missile site?

JP: There were eight of us that managed to get together. We were
members of the Atlantic Life Community, which is a series of
communities involved in peace actions up and down the Atlantic
coast. We got to know each other through peace actions at the
Pentagon and other places. Soon after that, we started spending
weekends with each other, exploring possibilities of engaging in a
direct action together. We would find a church to spend the weekend in, bring a lot of food and spend two or three days talking about
the proposed action, talking about our feelings, our convictions, our
doubts and fears. We were trying to see what this would mean for
us on a personal level, as well as trying to build up a degree of
trust between ourselves.

CT: After that you decided to go to Orlando?

JP: We met about every other weekend for four months. We only decided where we were going to go and what we were going to do at the very end of this period. We decided we wanted to focus our action on the Pershing II missile because that was the missile of the moment, as far as NATO deployments were concerned. Of course, it still is a beast. The Pershing was made in Orlando, so that is why we went there. Some of us hitch-hiked. Two of us took a plane and the others carpooled. When we arrived in Orlando, there were people who very generously helped us in faith, even though it was a great risk for them to do so.

CT: Then came Easter Sunday [1984], which was on April 22. Coincidentally, it happened to be my 40th birthday. I regard your action, by the way, as the best possible birthday present. So, on Easter Sunday, what took place?

JP: In the early hours after midnight, we had a short period of silence together in the house. Then we got into two cars and went to the Martin Marietta nuclear weapon base. We were carrying a bolt cutter, hammers, crowbars, bottles of blood and documents. We quietly unloaded them out of the cars and went through the woods along a path we had scoped out another day. We then hid ourselves in the bushes near the back of a building that was called the Pershing Missile Kit Building. We didn't have any inside contacts at the Martin Marietta plant. All we knew was that there was this building called the Pershing Missile Kit Building. It sounded like that would be where they were shipping those things out of. So we hid out there for about an hour while the mosquitoes and the chiggers [a kind of tick] did their number on us. We watched for guards and didn't see any.

CT: What time was this?

JP: It was about four in the morning. Then we crept up to the fence, applied the bolt cutter and entered the base. We broke into two groups. One of us pried the door open in the Pershing Kit Building and went inside. One of these kits, which was in a huge box, was used to convert Pershing I missiles into Pershing II missiles. We chose one of about 40 boxes and opened it, took parts out and began to destroy them. We hung a banner in the building saying 'Violence ends where love begins.' We hung pictures of children and loved ones around.

The other group went to some Pershing II launchers, which are like huge trucks. They climbed onto one of the launchers and cut the hydroylic and electrical cables. In a yard full of these launchers, they chose one, made it so that it couldn't be used, put a banner on it and poured blood on it. Then we all came back to a very obvious spot in front of the Pershing Kit Building, sat in a circle on top of some pallets and waited to be discovered.

CT: Given all the paranoia with regard to terrorists, your lives must have been very much at risk. You could have all been shot at any time while inside this missile factory. How were you working with all that fear?

JP: Yeah, fear and also wondering whether this was a very smart thing to be doing. [Laughter] We had to ask ourselves how would we feel if just one of our number was wounded or killed. What would the effect be on the person who did the deed? Would it have all been worth the risk? When the guards came, we were all holding hands in a circle. We left our hammers and crowbars far away. We were sitting in a circle and we began singing, 'Peace is flowing like a river.'

CT: What was the response of the guards? They saw you sitting there as a group in the middle of the night singing and their missiles having been hammered.

JP: The first person who might have seen us was driving by in a car, quite close by. He almost came over to us and then sped off. We didn't see anything more for about 15 minutes. The second guard that came up was a woman, an Israeli woman, and her reaction when she saw us was to say, 'My God, what are you doing here?' She had sincere wonder in her voice, not so much concern or fear. She stayed near by. She left her gun in her holster and got on her car radio and called for reinforcements. They began to arrive in great numbers from many different police agencies.

CT: And they took you away? Where did they take you to?

JP: They left us there for another two or three hours while they checked out the scene. The Martin Marietta executives came and looked over the mess. We were taken away from the group one by one and questioned, all very politely, remarkably politely, and then they let us go back onto our pallet to sit down in our circle. About another three hours later, we were arrested and taken to the Orange County jail. This was a nasty place. The cell that I was in for a month before the trial was 10 by 14 feet. There were eight men in this cell and we only got out for an hour a day to eat. There was no exercise period. There was no sorting of criminals. There were people in the cell on traffic violations and there were rapists.

CT: Were you handcuffed at all?

JP: Yes. After we were finally arrested there was all of that heavy steel kind of stuff. That lasted from then until the time we got to Danbury Prison in September. We had a lot of legal points we wanted to make at the trial and we weren't able to say very many of them. We wanted to make the argument that these weapons were illegal. We brought an indictment of the Martin Marietta Corporation and the United States Government into the action with us, making the point that these weapons have no right to exist by law.

CT: By whose law?

JP: By international law and also by Judeo-Christian law. The trial lasted six days. We were going to make the argument that we have a human right to act against these weapons because these weapons endanger life. It's a legal principle analogous to breaking into a burning house to rescue the children that are on the second story. There are various legal standards that you have to meet to make this argument. We worked hard to meet them but we didn't get a chance. We were not allowed to bring in expert witnesses, including lawyers, historians and biologists who would testify as to the imminent danger of nuclear weapons.

CT: What were you actually charged with?

JP: We were charged with conspiracy and destruction of US Government property. The jury took about an hour to eat lunch and find us guilty. We were all given the same sentence by the judge – three years.

CT: That seems like a very tough sentence! In Europe, there have been break-ins at nuclear bases, such as when the women broke in at Greenham Common. They have generally been given seven or fourteen days in prison. In West Germany, there was a fine and no prison sentence when peace activists were arrested after cutting through the fence.

JP: Yes, and there have been harder ones. Ours was the eighth in the series of Plowshare actions. The ninth of the series happened in Minneapolis at the Sperry Rand Company. Two people went in and smashed a prototype computer that was being built as part of a missile guidance system. These people were tried and convicted and given a six months suspended sentence by the judge. He gave a very interesting opinion. He said there is some kind of strange double standard going on here. The judge had just previously heard a case where Sperry Rand had been taken to court by the government for a three million dollar overcharge on one contract. The government had asked that the Sperry Rand Company pay back 10 per cent of that money to the government who hadn't sought any prosecution for any of the executives. So the judge was wondering what was going on here because the US attorney wanted to throw these two young peace activists away [imprison them].

CT: What happened at other Plowshare actions?

JP: The tenth in the series was in Providence, Rhode Island. People went into the Electric Boat Shipyard and hammered on D-5 missile tubes. This D-5 missile system will be going into the new Trident submarines. It's going to transform these weapons from retaliatory weapons into first strike weapons. These weapons are going to be extremely accurate. The activists have not been tried yet.

The eleventh break-in was at a Minuteman missile silo in Kansas by four people: Helen Woodson, who incidentally adopted 10 children with Down's Syndrome, Carl and Paul Kabat, brothers who were also priests, and an American Indian named White Feather. Carl spent a lot of time doing work among the poor in Peru and Chile, and his brother worked in American cities. The four of them walked one night through the corn fields pulling a 90-pound jack hammer and air compressor, broke through the fence and went to work on the lid of this missile silo.

They were very recently tried and convicted. Helen and Carl were given EIGHTEEN-YEAR SENTENCES. Paul was given a TEN-YEAR SENTENCE and White Feather was given an EIGHT-YEAR SENTENCE for this protest which did a total of $11,000 damage.

CT: That seems to me a savage and barbaric sentence. Why isn't there a great deal of publicity about it? Four people committed no violence to anybody and did a trivial amount of damage to US government property. Why is there no public outcry?

JP: It's not for lack of people trying to get it publicized. It did receive a little publicity in a Kansas City newspaper. This is the pattern of the way these actions get publicized. The first one, the Plowshares Eight, which involved Daniel and Philip Berrigan, did get some nationwide publicity. The other actions have had local publicity only. News items go out on the AP wire and UPI wire. Sometimes the hometown paper will pick up the story. The *New York Times* said nothing about the action out in Kansas, or the trial, or the sentence. The trial lasted for four days.

CT: Are the actions likely to continue considering quite a number of you are already in prison? Has the shock of this eighteen-year sentence really frightened other peace activists?

JP: I don't really know. The twelfth of these actions happened during the Kansas trial, in Kansas, when a man from Vermont, who was acting alone, hammered a Minuteman Missile silo. He will go to trial in the same courtroom. We are all very much with him. Clearly, the authorities are trying to deter these actions. They have decided that this has to stop. We have every reason to believe that the Justice Department does speak to the prosecutors and to the judges and there does seems to be a kind of national policy on how to deal with these actions. I think this last sentencing shows the heavy hand of Edwin Meese. Whether it will work or not, we will have to wait and see.

CT: Are you in prison with any of the others with whom you engaged in the action?

JP: There are four of us in the Danbury Prison Camp, two from the Griffiths Plowshares – the action that immediately preceded ours at a Strategic Air Command Base in Rome, New York. These people went into a hangar and hammered on a B-52 bomber that was being converted to carry air-launch Cruise Missiles. One of the people who engaged in that action was Elizabeth McAllister, one of the members of my community, along with Phil Berrigan's wife. She is in Alderson Prison in West Virginia now on a three-year sentence. Two of the men from that action are in Danbury Prison plus Todd Kaplan, my co-defendent and me. A fifth member of our group, Per Herngren, a Swedish national, is in heavy security because he is a foreigner.

CT: Are there any others in prison through heavy-handed treatment by the government?

JP: C. W. Deaton. He's a Texan and born-again Christian. He's imprisoned with us at Danbury. He's serving a fifty-year sentence. Yes, fifty years, for defying the Russian grain embargo. This embargo was a bad idea anyway. He is hoping to get pardoned one day. So far he's served nine years of his sentence.

CT: The peace movement tends to flow in waves of energy and enthusiasm and then it reaches a trough. In your time in prison, have you given much thought to new ways of expressing protest? And how can those of us who are not in prison contribute to the peace movement?

JP: We are interested in civil disobedience. We think it is very important to say, 'No!' in a very strong way to the politicians and the nuclear armament industry. Christian people tend to say, 'Not in My Name.' For me, 'Not in My Name' means not in the name of humanity.

CT: In prison, are there any restrictions on your expression? Can you have letters going out or coming in?

JP: There are restrictions on books. They can do what they want with our mail but the mail comes and goes very easily as far as I can see. Nothing that I've sent out has been censored. All the incoming mail is opened, but I don't know if it is really read.

CT: Where does much of your mail go?

JP: A lot of it goes to Florida. 'Swords into Plowshares' is our slogan. We saw the sword as the Pershing missile and the plowshare is the peace community in Florida. When we look for results, that's what we look for. We did leave an invigorated peace community in Florida.

CT: Some Christians view the missiles as an idol.

JP: American nuclear policy is a state religion. These weapons are modern idols. It is up to us to smash them. One of the arguments that we are trying to get into court is that we can't live with American nuclear policy and at the same time claim to have any right to practise our religion.

CT: Is the argument that these missiles deny true religious feelings and expression being heard by the courts?

JP: Liz McAllister began to work on it for the Griffiths trial and a refinement was brought to the Second Circuit Court of Appeals in New York. One of our friends is Ramsey Clark, who was the

Attorney General under Johnson. He's taken part in many noble causes and has a great deal of hope for this argument. He thinks that over the years this will be the important legal argument.

Nuclear missiles are clearly illegal under international law and under the Nuremberg principles. As individuals, we have the right and responsibility to act against our government when it is acting illegally. We want this argument heard in court. So far the judges have said, 'We're not going to hear that argument.' But the judge in Syracuse said, 'That's an interesting argument. Someday some judge is going to hear it but it's not going to be me.'

CT: The government may have to start listening to the various forms of sustained protest taking place via the courts. Presumably that is part of the motive of those who engaged in such peace actions.

JP: It's a tough issue for the peace movement. Some people believe in the courts and some don't. When we get together in our communities, the communities will almost always break down into those who want to do a sophisticated legal defence and those who think that the courts are hopeless and would simply like to speak the truth, forgetting about legal form. Our friends in Kansas City who got eighteen-year terms were among those who thought you can't talk to these people in their language. They just spoke the truth as they saw it in a very powerful and eloquent way. But they did not follow legal form, which, by the way, makes it very difficult for them to appeal.

CT: Have they decided to appeal? I know that Helen, who has the eighteen-year sentence, wrote to you. What is she experiencing at this time?

JP: She's being held under harsh circumstances, but nevertheless, is experiencing joy and community. There was no precedent for the eighteen-year term. However, she has made no compromises with the prison authorities and has denied all offers to help her receive clemency. In her view the monstrosity of nuclear weapons dwarfs the injustice to her, and they are the issue. She doesn't want anyone to make *her* the issue. 'Don't worry about me,' she writes, 'abolish the weapons.'

CT: In other words, she has chosen to keep her faith; not to have faith in the legal system. In what ways is she being supported?

JP: We have a Peace Prisoners' Fast on the first day of every month in the various prisons around the country. All of us who were involved in these actions fast. We ask other people who are interested to join with us. Also, there is a woman who takes our writings and sends them out to the local peace newsletters and the local groups around the country. Each one of our groups has a support committee which publishes a newsletter and sends money for the prisoners' commissary funds, if necessary, or to help out the families.

CT: It seems important to bring the attention of as many people as possible to the situation that you are all in, especially those who were sentenced in Kansas. This is repression. The sentence is totally out of touch with the offence.

Before we end, is there anything else that you would like to add?

JP: I'm all talked out!

CT: I would like to express my deep appreciation to you for your concern, your courage and to all those who are saying 'No!' in such a clear and direct way. May these contributions to peace and justice make inroads into the minds of people in government. One more question: How are your five children handling their dad being in prison?

JP: They think it's great!

The religion of consumerism

An interview with Sulak Sivaraksa
Bangkok, Thailand

In August 1984 Sulak Sivaraksa, Thailand's internationally respected activist for peace and social justice, was arrested by the Thai government on charges of lese-majeste (offending the Thai monarch) for comments he made in an interview. It was during a period of martial law in the country.

There was an international outcry over his arrest. Amnesty International, peace organizations, aid agencies, religious leaders, universities and lawyers around the world and in Thailand protested vigorously.

Sulak made statements in the taped interview such as, 'I think the king should be looked upon as a human being who exercises his power judiciously but is nevertheless fallible. If I wish to attack the ninth king, I must write during the reign of the ninth king. I don't have to wait for the next.'

In a country where there is reverence for king, country and religion, Sulak's comments were seemingly used as an opportunity to silence his voice. After his arrest he was held for twelve days in a top-security detention centre. He was due to be tried in a military court and faced between three and thirty years imprisonment. There would be no appeal after sentencing and observers would not be permitted to witness the trial.

Commenting on the international response, the Thai interior minister said at the time: 'The law is Thai law. Foreigners must not interfere with our judicial process.'

On 30 November, Sulak and two co-defendants, the interviewer and publisher, appeared in court and were informed by the presiding judge that the public prosecutors wished to withdraw the case.

Afterwards Sulak said, 'It was a good period to test my spiritual strength and to learn to appreciate one's friends and well-wishers, both at home and abroad. Prayers were said for us regularly by

Buddhists, Christians, Hindus and Muslims. We must really help other victims of injustice as we all live on this tiny planet Earth.'

Sulak Sivaraksa, 55, married with three children, is a lawyer, social analyst, non-violent campaigner, lecturer and educationalist. He is the co-ordinator of the Asian Cultural Forum on Development and chairperson for the Thai Inter-Religious Commission of Development. He is a member of the international board of the Buddhist Peace Fellowship. He has had a number of books published in English, including *Siamese Resurgence, A Buddhist Vision for Renewing Society*, and *Siam Through a Looking Glass: a Critique*.

Sulak interprets the contemporary crisis in both spiritual and social terms. He speaks out against corruption, communism, nationalism, capitalism and consumerism. He speaks for the renewal of the countryside, the value of constructive criticism, the necessity to support and protect the poor and the application of Buddhist principles to social reality.

Not surprisingly, he has been in trouble regularly with the authorities over the years. In 1976 while speaking overseas, he read in *The Times* newspaper in England of a warrant out in Thailand for his arrest. At the time, during a military takeover, his bookshop in the heart of Bangkok and right opposite his home was raided by the police and army, accompanied by television and press crews. Thousands of his books were burnt, rendering him almost bankrupt.

At the present time in Thailand there is a fledgling kind of democracy and greater opportunity to write and speak one's mind. The authorities and Thai society seem to be developing a begrudging appreciation of Sulak's outspokenness. One person said of Sulak: 'Sulak is like a gadfly in the ear of the government.' (Throughout many changes in government, King Bhumipol of Thailand has to his credit constantly maintained contact with his people by spending months of the year visiting the rural areas listening to their voices of concern, taking notes on the spot and telling politicians and civil servants what he hears.)

I met with Sulak at his home in Bangkok, where he has lived for the past forty years. While we met, there were many visitors. He had just arranged for a small party of monks and lay people to travel to Sri Lanka to speak against violence and to raise more voices for non-violence in the conflict between the Sinhalese and Tamils.

CT: In recent years you have seen the enormous impact of Western consumerism on Thai society. Since you have lived in both England and Thailand and have some awareness about the Western culture, please say a little about the impact.

SS: You must realize that Thailand, which I prefer to call Siam, was not colonized, which is a blessing. But we have been more harmed than those countries which became colonies of the West. At least our neighbour Burma, which was colonized, resists Western consumerism. Unfortunately, Thailand never resisted the West because we thought that we maintained our independence. First we were colonized intellectually by adopting a Western way of living but we still preserved our political independence. At first these Western intellectual colonizations only took place among the Thai elite in Bangkok. The rest of the country was more or less free from this form of Western colonization, partly due to Buddhism and partly to our indigenous culture.

CT: When did this influence of Western intellectualism begin in Bangkok?

SS: Sir John Bowden came here in 1855. He forced the open door policy and so we signed the Bowden Treaty with England. King Mongut, internationally known in *The King and I*, was a Buddhist monk for 26 years. He was wise because if we did not open our country we would be colonized by the British. So he opened the country to the British. At the same time he invited the French, Swedish and Germans to balance the situation. So politically, although we were not equal to the West, we felt superior to our neighbours who were colonized by the French, British, Dutch and Americans. Our first downfall was to look down upon our neighbours. We thought we were equal to the West. In fact, we wanted to be equal to the West, so gradually we followed the West. We invited the English lady, Miss Anna Leonowens, to teach children here. King Chulalonkorn sent all his sons to be educated abroad. When they came back they still retained their Buddhist heritage and Thai culture but they admired the Western way of life. They gradually introduced Western education, medicine, technology and administration. Correspondingly, this reduced our indigenous education and culture. Buddhism as the state religion became formal like the Church of England and it lost much of its sanctity.

CT: There has been an acceleration of the values of consumerism in the last twenty years . . .

SS: . . . thirty years. At least the old culture maintained a certain *noblesse oblige* but the new elite, devoid of the old culture, just want to be rich and powerful in the name of development. They just want to expand in every direction, including cutting the country up through road building. In the old colonial system the British and the French tried to maintain themselves. They thought they would be in this part of the world forever. On the one hand they had to respect us, and on the other hand, they had to maintain the environmental balance. The West thought it could get our timbers for ever. They replanted the trees so there was not much destruction of the forests. But then the Americans came. They have a very short-term view. They wanted to get the natural wealth of the country out as quickly as possible. The American period coincided with the development of Bangkok and the rest of the country. With the American period came the age of advertisement – the age of the consumer culture which claims to be a universal culture. So a decadent Western culture was brought to Thailand alongside sexism, violence and the use of drugs by the young. If you come to Bangkok now you can see the new kind of temple in the form of a department store. People flock there.

CT: Bangkok looks just like any Western city. One goes outside of Bangkok and one can still sense rural Thai society. Is the shadow of Bangkok penetrating into the rural traditions?

SS: Yes, unfortunately. Development is another word for greed. Our city people never owned land up country. We never had absentee landlords before. In this age of so-called development the developers want more land and so destroy more forest. Our education teaches people to admire the urban life, the civil service and business. So obviously we brain-drain our rural areas. If you go to the villages today you find old people. The young, who have mental power and ambition, are leaving the villages for Bangkok. If you cannot compete in Bangkok you may go to the Middle East to sell your labour. We even export our women as prostitutes to Germany, Japan and Hong Kong. The minds and bodies of the young are exploited.

CT: These are all signs of the erosion of a society. Isn't there a danger of idealizing traditional rural society and values and seeing all the fault in Western consumerism and its values?

SS: There is a danger if you romanticize it. Rural society was not all that ideal but it was self-sustaining. People respected one another; the young respected the old. In every Thai village there was a temple which was a centre for spiritual, educational and cultural activities. The self-supporting village had been functioning for at least 700 years in this way. It wasn't ideal but it worked. The Buddhist philosophy has as a central principle that it is noble to give rather than take. We may not be very good Buddhists but we practised generosity [*dana* in Pali, the early Buddhist language]. We offer what we can to each other. We use the word *sahnuk*, which means to enjoy our life in a relaxed way. In the traditional Thai culture play and work is part of life; competition is not to be admired but co-operation is. This approach worked. In this view those who lived a virtuous and ethical way of life, like the monks, were very much appreciated. At the same time there was respect for other life forms such as animals, birds, fish and trees. Within my lifetime there has been this major change.

CT: Why is it that self-supporting, self-sustaining societies have simply not been able to withstand the pressure of consumerism and that consumerism becomes the predominant religion? Why is consumerism so powerful that it eats into every worthwhile value?

SS: You have got to realize that consumerism represents greed. We all have greed within ourselves. Consumerism is basically linked with feelings of power, elitism, and a sophisticated kind of education in science and technology. In fact, power represents aggression and anger and we all have that. The new educational system teaches you to be clever but not wise. In fact, we create delusion in ourselves and we think that it is knowledge. Unless we understand the root causes of greed, aggression and self-delusion we get bogged down. Consumer society works like magic on the mind. It deceives you into believing in the value of consuming more, going faster, living in greater convenience. It sounds wonderful but you do not realize the cost. I feel that once people realize the negative aspects then the situation can change.

CT: Are people realizing the negative aspects?

SS: One of the good things about this country is that more and more people are realizing this. There are positive aspects to the consumer society but there seem to be more negative aspects. Once we realize this we can resist it.

CT: There are then two realizations. One is the force of greed, aggression and delusion and the second is the realization of the impact these forces have on society and the planet.

SS: Being a Buddhist, I have to see everything with *upaya*, that is, with skilful means. The Buddha taught that the first thing to be aware of is *dukkha*, unsatisfactoriness, or suffering. Once you understand that consumerism brings *dukkha*, you find the causes for *dukkha*.

CT: The friend who drove the Venerable Nagasena, the Venerable Pannavuddho [two Buddhist monks] and I here today is a business-man in Bangkok. He was cheated two years ago by a business partner of one million baht [£20,000]. He is still suffering today over the situation.

SS: Unless the man looks into himself and into the causes, the suffering continues. You have to translate the essential teaching from your spiritual tradition to confront the modern period. Other-wise, Buddhism is nothing more than a decoration, which most governments would like it to be. Paying respect to the national religion and holding big ceremonies may be useful but at the same time could be more harmful. We can apply the skilful means of the Buddha to understand suffering and social reality and the way to be free from suffering. Through mindfulness, non-violence and Buddhist practices, there is the possibility of overcoming suffering, both personally and socially.

CT: What are the skilful means for social change?

SS: The good thing about this country is that it has been a Buddhist kingdom for a long, long time and is one of the few left. The Buddhist heritage is available in almost every village, although many villages have succumbed and only the form is left. But there are still many villages which have the form, content and local spiritual leadership. I know this country. I live in the capital. I have also been exposed to the West. My job is to tell people of the ways available to overcome their suffering and the unsatisfactoriness in life. I work on myself and my society. I look to spiritual leaders, who have mindfulness and awareness themselves. I have met quite a few who try to have a positive answer.

CT: Can you give me an example of engaged spiritual leadership?

SS: In Surin province in the north-east of Thailand [the poorest region of the country], an abbot remembered that when he was young, people were also poor but he sensed that there was more happiness at that time. The people related to each other much better and there was that *sahnuk* feeling among the people. In the environment, there was plenty of jungle and the elephants roamed the region freely. The people were free and were able to rely on themselves and the environment. They produced food for their families and for the monks and nuns. What was left over, they sold. They had the four prerequisites of food, clothing, shelter and medicine. In the last thirty years, through constant development there are more highways and roads. The jungle has disappeared, the elephants have disappeared, except for the elephants kept for the tourist to photograph. The people suffer.

CT: What is the abbot's response to all this impact upon Surin?

SS: The abbot said that something is seriously wrong. Consumerism means capitalism; it means money comes first. 'Our local resources go to Bangkok, the multinational corporations and then to the superpowers,' he said. 'This is useless and wasteful.' He felt that there must be a way to confront things together and solve things together. He said that we must use the old traditions.

CT: Are people expressing interest in that approach?

SS: Oh yes. This is a success story. When he started, people didn't believe him, but being a monk and meditation master they would come. He pointed out to them what went wrong. He said, 'Let's try alternative ways of living.' He even used strong words like 'communal farming'. In this country consumerism came along with anti-communism. If you use such concepts as communalism or communal farming here then you can be accused of being a communist. But when a monk who is pure in conduct of body, speech and mind speaks this way, he arouses interest among the people.

CT: Obviously the role of the monk is important in terms of renewal of deeper human values.

SS: The old customs and values must be translated into the contemporary setting. Today people are suffering a great deal. People were told that their traditional values were no good. They were told not to use the buffalo for farming but instead use the tractors. People were fascinated with technology. Hired labour occurred with bigger farms instead of small self-sufficient competitiveness and therefore, brought more and more suffering to village life. The monk said that the people have been brainwashed into this way of thinking and living.

CT: What alternatives is he suggesting?

SS: He is encouraging the people to farm together, to share their labour together and join together. Skilful means has also to be applied to every area of rural life including the shortage of rice, the unpredictable weather and the destruction of the jungle and forests. The abbot said we need to have a rice bank instead of going to the bank to borrow money. The temples can start the rice bank – whatever is cultivated and left over from eating is offered to the temple. The temple keeps the grain. Anybody in need receives the grain from the temple free of charge. It is a new kind of merit-making translated straight away into social reality.

CT: How do the people respond to this?

SS: Very well. The temple has become powerful and serviceable to the people. The next project the abbot started was a buffalo bank. Being Buddhists, we don't like to kill the buffalo. The temple keeps the buffalos and offers the offspring of the buffalo to the people who can't afford to buy them. The condition is that the buffalo must be treated kindly. Half of any future offspring which comes must be returned to the buffalo bank.

Up until 1973 we were told that we were the last of the free lands. We had to fight the communists and believe in Americanism and consumerism. We had been brainwashed for so long. Young people started questioning that. In 1973 the students rejected the American model but unfortunately they went to the other extreme, to the Maoist model. So we were in danger of jumping from the frying pan into the fire. Hence, in 1976 the military came back into power with the blessings of the Americans and Japanese and began killing our students. Other students fled to the jungle. Others joined the Communist Party of Thailand under the influence of the Communist Party of China. That bitter lesson taught the students that Communism was not the answer; it was a fake. They have come to see that the social way of life of their ancestors and what the

Buddha taught is truly meaningful and can be applied in the present time.

CT: You are speaking of the Middle Way – between the two extremes of capitalism and communism.

SS: That's right. We must turn the society towards social justice. We must change both ourselves and our society. There are, of course, monks not in touch with the modern world, both in a positive and negative way. Sometimes when they are not in touch they have insight and wisdom to give us. Others who are not in touch with the world hang on to outdated ceremonies. Again we have to use skilful means to distinguish the sheep from the goats.

CT: You have been consistently outspoken in your public lectures, meetings and writings. How free is free speech in Thailand today?

SS: To be fair to the government, compared with all our neighbours in south-east Asia, we are much more free. We can speak our mind on almost any subject, except perhaps the monarchy.

CT: Did you tread on the toes of the government when you voiced criticisms in 1984? What you said and wrote brought you before the military court.

SS: The pretext was that I said something against the monarchy. I feel if the monarchy is to survive it has got to survive like the Western kind of monarchy. It is not that I admire the Western monarchy, but I think it survived because it could withstand criticism. To me criticism is an essential teaching of the Buddha. I criticize the Buddha too. The Buddha welcomed criticism of him and his teaching. He instructs that we do not accept anything unless we scrutinize it.

CT: In a healthy society criticism must go into every area, even those areas regarded as sacred.

SS: I don't accept sacredness, you see. As a Buddhist, I revere the Buddha more than anybody else. Even so, he is not sacred. I respect him profoundly but even his teachings should be criticized.

CT: In the time you faced charges for your criticism of the monarchy there was a strong protest from the West over the charges.

SS: To be fair, the King was also a little bit embarrassed. He was educated in Switzerland. He is a man who would welcome criticism personally.

CT: He does tremendous work for the rural people and the hill tribes.

SS: Without doubt, he has very good intentions, but with some of his good intentions I disagree. We should be able to spell out differences openly.

CT: You have spoken in this interview about what has happened to Bangkok. Why do you choose personally to live in Bangkok? Why aren't you living in a rural society?

SS: Partly my own roots are here in the city. Former generations of my family were in Bangkok. I feel that my role is as an urban person. I can learn from the rural area for the benefit of Bangkok and I feel that Bangkok is the place where we suck everything from other areas. We must change the people of Bangkok so that they respect the people in the rural areas. That's my job. As part of my job as co-ordinator of the Asian Forum and Development I had to work in the whole region. I feel that if you want social justice in any village you can't do it in one village. The work has to be linked to other villages; one country has to be linked with other countries; the Third World has to be linked with the First World. We have to build up that understanding and use the Buddhist methodology of *kalyana mitta*, that is, good friends, who are on a similar wavelength and have a similar understanding. We must help each other. The small fishermen must help the working women; the working women must help industrial workers. Somehow we must all start relating to each other.

CT: Are there *any* messages coming from the West which are valuable and healthy? Does the West have any part to play in the so-called Third World?

SS: The good thing about the West is that it is now realizing the harmfulness that it has done. This is a very good sign. A monk who has committed harmful acts must ask for forgiveness. Since the 18th century and the Age of Enlightenment, the West has believed it has had the answers. The West believed it must conquer everybody else and nature too. Now more people in the West are saying, 'No, our knowledge is limited. Our thought does not go very far at all.' I think that is very profound. I think awareness and understanding will help Thailand and other countries tremendously. The West is just starting to become humble. More people in the

West want to learn from our rural cultures. This is wonderful. Second, the West is beginning to explore spiritual depths, not only appreciating Buddhism but also inquiring into its own Christian background. Christian mystics have very profound things to say to us which the West has denied in the last 200 or 300 years.

CT: What else do you appreciate from the West at the present time?

SS: The West has developed a certain kind of method and organization as a kind of network which we must learn. For example, the Christians have the World Council of Churches which brings together Christian activists from around the world. We have the World Fellowship of Buddhists but it is just a kind of club. The West is willing to confront the power blocks like the multinational corporations. This is wonderful. We must learn to organize ourselves in this way, too.

CT: What would you say the West must truly learn about itself?

SS: The West has to learn how to relate truly in an equal way to the rest of the world. The West must recognize that it has a lot to learn from the rest of the world as much as we have to learn from the West.

CT: You are saying that there is an opportunity for fresh forms of dialogue, not based on a colonial and patronizing attitude?

SS: This is very essential. I feel my own drawback. I don't know the Middle East and yet I would like to. I would like to learn from the Muslims. I have learnt from Indonesia, which is Muslim and nearer to us. Certain sections of the Muslim community there have inherited from the Buddhist tradition. We related together quite closely. We have to learn in this day and age from each other.

CT: As an organizer of spiritual and social activism, how do you get by financially? Who gives you the funds?

SS: When you organize at the national and international level the money comes from the West, mostly from Christian organizations. European Catholics and Protestants have been generous. I tried unsuccessfully to get some funds from the Buddhists of Japan. Fortunately, we have been able to raise more money within Thailand itself. People usually make merit here by giving money to the temples, but too much money is spent on building temples and on useless ceremonies. People are collecting money for increasing social awareness and understanding. I hope that in a decade all the money will come from within Thailand.

CT: That will be another expression of being self-supporting.

SS: Yes, that's right . . . I am very glad to talk with you. You are an example of bridging our part of the world with the Western part. You came to learn from us and you also come to teach us. I think that this is a very good new dimension. It must be developed further.

The Price of poverty

An interview with Mary Lightfoot
Bodh Gaya, Bihar, India

When I arrived in Bodh Gaya in Bihar, India, regarded as one of the poorest, most corrupt and most violent places in India, I was hoping to meet with Mary Lightfoot immediately. However, I was told by a friend that she had to dash off to Varanasi three days ago. There had been a terrible accident.

It turned out that Vikasbhai, 48, an internationally known social activist and consultant for aid agencies, had been killed in an accident. He had been travelling in his jeep in Maharashtra, India, with a close German family and their two children, who he loved as his own. Tragically, to the deep sorrow of the parents, Vikas and both children were killed.

Vikas, who had been associated with Oxfam and other aid agencies for more than twenty years, had helped establish projects to help the very poor in many regions of India. In a tribute, the *Oxfam News*, the journal of the agency, said, 'What made him so memorable was his capacity for friendship with all whom he dealt, the warmth of his welcome to the many who visited what he liked to call his "elastic" house in Varanasi.'

Vikas was a friend and advisor to Mary. She would draw on his broad experience to help guide her in her role as an independent voluntary social worker. The support system for field workers is a vital aspect, since the work demands effective and responsible action.

Mary Lightfoot, 42, was born into a Roman Catholic family in Victoria, Australia where she studied and worked as a pharmacist. She travelled extensively from her early twenties, living and working in England and other European countries. In the early 1970s she went to India and has since spent more time there than anywhere else. She decided to become involved in social work with the poor and under-privileged, and learnt Hindi so that she could communicate directly with the people. Her long stay in and around Bodh Gaya, a main centre of pilgrimage for Buddhists and Hindus, eventually brought her to the notice of various authorities, including police and politicians.

As with any such undertaking, once one is identified with a particular group, it is likely to produce resentment and hostility from others. At times Mary has received criticism from the powerful because of her support for the powerless. But the Indian Government seems to appreciate her work as she has been given the necessary visa extensions.

The death of Vikas may well mark a further turning point in her work because of the probability of having to extend herself in order to be one of the support figures for the small groups of field workers in Eastern U.P. and Bihar. They have the task of trying to fill the gap left by Vikas.

Not surprisingly, Mary looked quite tired when she returned from her twelve-day visit to Varanasi. She had been there to comfort friends and family, and to participate in meetings as to how to carry on Vikas' work. As she said, 'When a social worker like Vikas dies, thousands of lives are directly affected.'

CT: You have been based here in Bodh Gaya since 1980. Why did you decide to stay in this region?

ML: It happened organically. When I came back to India for the third time I intended to stay on and get involved with the people in some useful way. I had a list of places that I wanted to check out. One of them was in Bodh Gaya, an ashram which was doing work in some villages in the area. Immediately after sitting the Bodh Gaya retreat with you, I went to stay in this ashram, with an English social worker who was already there. We engaged in health work, which is my training and background, with the fifty girls who were living there. We also helped in the kitchen and the garden and did much of the office work for the child sponsorship programme operating through there. We worked with the ashram for about eighteen months, some of that time living in a tiny village seven miles from Bodh Gaya.

CT: How did you support yourself?

ML: For a few months the ashram provided our basic food needs. I had some money which I had saved in the West and my family was supportive. The money to buy medicine and other needs for our work came from my Aunt Louise, who had spent many years in India. The money which she left to my father after she died has been used towards village development work here. Since a first 'appeal' letter to friends and relatives in 1980, I have not had to ask for money. There always seems to be enough for what needs to be done.

CT: Where did the fifty girls come from who were living in the ashram?

ML: They came from a few surrounding villages, from the lower strata of harijans ('Children of God' – Gandhi's name for the outcastes). Mostly they came because of their severe poverty, not because their families wanted to get rid of them. Most of the villages that the ashram works with are virtually one caste. They are new villages, situated on Bhoodan land. In the 1950s Vinoba Bhave and others walked throughout much of India, asking for land from the landlords, to be distributed to the landless. This was called *bhoodan* (land gift) land.

CT: What difference does it make to have one caste rather than a collection of castes?

ML: Almost all villages are multi-caste. Many castes create many divisions in the society, from the higher castes, which include the landlords, to the lower castes who provide services to the landlords, such as washing and cleaning. It still is a feudal system in many ways. These bhoodan villages are unusual in being one caste. Most of the people resettled in them were once bonded labourers to the landlords, so it meant a new start in their lives.

CT: What were the aims of the ashram in working with these people?

ML: The professed aims of the ashram were to assist the people to be able to lead a better life, and through the ashram schools to give their children basic education and training to become leaders of their own people.

When I first came to the ashram my main interest was the welfare of the girls and I didn't want to know about the ashram politics. Since there had been a succession of foreign volunteers, information was passed on to me. We were doing office work and had access to letters and accounts, and close contact with members of the staff.

As time went by I simply had to take notice of what was going on there. I began to see how much corruption there was, how much exploitation of the people and their condition in order to get foreign money, which was then not being used in the way it was intended for by the donors. There were many ways of fiddling the accounts. All this got worse over the years till most of the money was being used by people who should not have had access to it at all, such as a woman who worked in the ashram, her relatives and her long-time boyfriend, a local politician.

CT: So why did you finally leave the ashram?

ML: After being away from Bodh Gaya one summer, I made the decision to work independently and not support what was going on at the ashram. I went to live in the Burmese Vihar instead of at the ashram. Doing this showed that I was still involved in the activities of the area, but I was not giving my support to that ashram, even though the people there asked me to come back and stay.

CT: Did the people in the villages want you? How did you gain their trust?

ML: We had gone out to the villages as visitors quite a few times from the beginning. One of the villages, in which we stayed, Baranamba, had a very high proportion of young women with young children in very poor health. They were malnourished, which is normal, and they also had widespread sores. During our ten-day stay, most of the children were healed or well on their way to being healed. Since we had such a short time, we had to use antibiotics. Some people wouldn't co-operate; they would not wash their children's bodies. And yet, many could see that something could be done and the women really wanted us back.

CT: Was it enough to provide medicine and keep the children washed?

ML: We tried to educate the villagers about diet, such as the value of eating green leaves and unpolished rice, both considered poor people's food, and we promoted use of simple home remedies.

The health problems are basic, namely poor hygiene and poor nutrition due to poverty and lack of education. I had enough background to treat a lot of illnesses. Here you can buy any medicine over the counter. I had studied homeopathic medicine with a Canadian friend in Almora [India] and I used that kind of treatment most of the time. We also did other relief and family welfare work and facilitated agricultural work, helping people to get supplies, or loans for pumps.

CT: In stepping out and being an independent social worker and having information about the ashram, couldn't that have jeopardized your position in the area? Wouldn't you be viewed with some suspicion?

ML: Rumours that I was a troublemaker were put out by the ashram, which did make it difficult. Also, the ashram made trouble for the villagers when I went out there. And there was jealousy because we would only treat the poor. Those who could afford to go to the doctor we would not treat. When the village situation improved because the people there got work with a cash income in the gravel factories in Gaya, the main town, I left the village. I then based myself in Bodh Gaya, which is basically a collection of small villages.

CT: What happens to a poor family that has no money or food? Does the village support the family?

ML: The family systems here are generally fairly close and supportive, but not always. It is amazing that some people manage to keep body and soul together and find food. For example, one woman that I know, named Urmilla, is in her mid-twenties. She has four children and is a widow. When we first knew her a few years ago, the youngest child was very close to death; they were in a very desperate situation. She used to go to Gaya to be with her mother and sometimes find domestic work. Her husband had become a *dacoit*, a robber, and was killed in a robbery. The people in the village just a few hundred yards from here said, 'Don't have anything to do with her. She's bad.' But the husband was the *dacoit*, not her. Urmilla lives next door to her in-laws, who harass her and others in the village.

By this time I was working with a Christian woman from Kerala who knows Bihar well. Once we had established trust with Urmilla, she really changed. When we first met her she was so fearful of what we would do to her. Now she has self-confidence. She is quite active in the village meetings and will speak out. She is very pretty and bright. The children go to school and her daughter is betrothed.

She now works with us when work is available, and she is very reliable and efficient.

CT: What has made the difference from being downtrodden and rejected as the wife of a *dacoit* to being a woman who is able to speak at village meetings?

ML: The fact that she respects herself and people respect her now. Unfortunately, there are very few examples like Urmilla. Most women are still in very bad positions. Overall, among the harijans, there is a change taking place, a growing political awareness. I have a number of young friends who are now working throughout this area, their home area, who are committed to informing the village people of their rights, such as education, land rights, and government subsidies, to which they are entitled. They want people to fight for their rights. They encourage non-violence, although there are forces that try to disrupt that.

CT: Who are the violent forces?

ML: The people who are in power locally are willing to use violence. One of our main opponents is the local politician. People around know he has power and how he uses it. He has a group of *goondas* [strong-arm men] who get the men in the village drunk so that he can influence them by fear and threats to do what he wants. He'll even give the villagers guns and ammunition to harass people whom he wants harassed. He can have people beaten up and murdered.

CT: Why?

ML: Because some of the people go against what he is trying to do. One of the problems someone like this man can cause, and this has happened to some friends of mine, is to start a false court case, e.g. by claiming that somebody stole something. The accused person will be arrested and jailed until bail is arranged and sometimes they receive a lot of harassment from the police. They will have to appear in court at least twice a month and get all the evidence together to prove their innocence. It costs them a lot of time and expense to keep going to the court, as well as the loss of work. Whatever they need in court, papers, and so forth, they must pay for, as well as the bribes to get anything done. The law and order mechanisms of the country are being used to harass and terrorize innocent people.

Then there is the well-known and documented Bodh Gaya land struggle, which has been going on for many years, with regard to land controlled by the Bodh Gaya *math* [Hindu monastery]. Fairly recently, the Supreme Court ruled that the *math* could only keep one hundred acres of land and yet the Bodh Gaya *math* was controlling over 12,000 acres. So there is a lot of land to be distributed and everybody wants it.

CT: How can the head of a *math* end up with 12,000 acres? It means that thousands of people are dispossessed in accordance to the number of acres he has. How is it that the people do not own the land they till?

ML: In many ways it is still a feudal society. Reforms did not touch India until after Independence in 1948. Laws have been passed with regard to land ownership – there are ceiling acts, but there are innumerable ways of getting around them because of corruption. For example, in the Bodh Gaya area, much of the land was parcelled out by the Hindu *math* not only in the name of disciples, but also in the name of deities!

CT: Technically, the land was not in a person's name, he had the land in the name of the various deities? Surely it is a clear-cut case?

ML: Just because a ruling is passed as a law of the land, does not make it happen. The Law here has very little impact on reality. Money is changing hands even in the courtroom.

In Urmilla's village, the people have been involved in this struggle for many years. People in the village were killed by police at the height of it. Since then, there have been many court cases going on. There are about 200 families in this village who have the right to some of this land. The hope was that each family would receive one acre. In fact, this village has only been allotted 60 acres to support 200 families.

CT: How did the villagers manage to get their case to the courts?

ML: They had the help of various Indian activists, including the Sangarsti Wahini of J.P. Naryan's movement. On their own, there is no way that they could have had the ability or know-how to start and continue legal action.

CT: Is the local politician doing anything?

ML: He has the ability to influence this land distribution and people are paying him to use his influence in their favour. Anybody who has money and wants this land is paying enormous bribes to people like him to get their hands on the land.

CT: What are the chances of the people in the village securing their 200 acres when they have only been allotted 60 acres?

ML: It is very hard to say. The people have said that they will not accept this offer and they will refuse to accept it until they are given their rights. There is a risk that they might lose the 60 acres.

CT: How does a village come to an agreement to fight? Some may say, 'Let's cut our losses and run,' while others might say that the village has the right to all of the land.

ML: That, of course, is happening. There are a few young activists working with the situation who have put a lot of energy and skill into organizing the village. Most of the decisions are made at meetings, which often go on all night. They work by concensus. Some of the activists are actually students who were educated by the ashram school that I was involved with. They were the best of the pupils. A handful of the hundreds who have gone through there are definitely gems. Of course, these activists are put down by the ashram since the local politician is part of the power structure of the ashram as well as one of its chief beneficiaries.

CT: It's ironic.

ML: It is ironic. It was the stated aim of the ashram earlier to educate some of the children to be leaders of their own people and now they are not given recognition for what they are doing, because it goes against the status quo. Instead, they are harassed and called antisocial elements by the institution which gave them basic education.

CT: Since you are familiar with the corruption, power and violence, why don't these corrupt people throw you out?

ML: The few people who control and benefit from the ashram have tried. They have tried very hard, but they haven't been able to achieve anything. Because of them I have been the subject of several police investigations but each time I'm investigated, I get better known and receive more respect from officials. One day I was shown a letter stating that my opponents had gone to the district police about me. Within a few hours, the head of the local police saw me in the street and said, 'If there is anything I can do for you, let me know. I am behind you and will support you in any way that I can.'

Soon after that, an official from Patna, the capital of Bihar, came here to meet me. He told me that the State Government had received a petition about me alleging that I was engaged in espionage against the country; agitating local labourers against local landowners; prostitution and procurement of foreign girls for prostitution; and illegal dealing in foreign goods, including narcotics. I asked him, 'Is that all?'

CT: What was the State Government's response to the allegations?

ML: This official said that he had made inquiries and had found no other complaints against me. I asked what his office would do about the matter. He answered, 'Just continue with what you're doing and don't worry. But you should be careful. There are obviously people in the area who wish you harm or don't want you here.'

CT: What do you see your role is within all that is going on around you?

ML: Well, I have to be very careful. I keep in the background with anything 'political' as far as possible. I act as part of a support system to some young activists – morally, emotionally and intellectually. I have access to knowledge, people and information which they may not have access to. I can help connect them with people they need to be in touch with. I know them well over many years. Now they are mostly independent and financially viable, but I still have contact with them. The force of their work will continue.

CT: For many Buddhists and pilgrims who come here, Bodh Gaya is the centre of the universe. It seems rather unfortunate that countless numbers of Asians and Westerners pass through without any real knowledge of the situation.

ML: So few people have much idea of what really goes on anywhere.

CT: In the beginning of the interview, you mentioned that you did the work of a child sponsorship programme in which Westerners act as kind of foster parents for poor children in the Third World. In the Australian press you have criticized these child sponsorship schemes. If people don't support these schemes, then what do you suggest?

ML: I suggest that people in the West inform themselves as much as possible about the Third World and about the aid agencies they are supporting. To give £10 or $20 a month (which is less than the price of a cup of coffee a day) is an easy way to assuage the guilt of affluent First Worlders and let them feel that they've done their bit. Rather than just send off a monthly cheque (or worse, have it debited to your account automatically), it is important for us to learn about the developing countries and, if possible, to visit them. Publications such as *New Internationalist* give a wide range of relevant information. It is important to give active support to aid and development agencies which work to increase public awareness of the daily lives and problems facing millions of people in other countries. The advertising, literature and correspondence of any aid agencies tell a lot of their ways of functioning and priorities and how they use the money they give.

CT: I have had thoughts of 'adopting' a child in the Third World. I thought it was a way for my daughter to sense the world as one huge family.

ML: Despite names like World Vision – one of the biggest 'multi-nationals of tear-trading', as Vikas called them – child sponsorship programmes give support to keeping people's vision narrow by not educating people to see the causes of poverty. There are a number of problems with the programmes. Benefits coming to one child, or one family, but not to the others cause division and jealousy within families and within communities. Child sponsorship programmes act to maintain the status quo and foster dependency rather than give a chance of real change. They encourage people to be passive and accept money and conditions rather than to stand up for their rights. They also tend to create unfulfillable desires and expectations in the sponsored children, resulting in discontent with their lives. At the same time, the children are trapped in an oppressed and exploitive system and they do not have the ability to get out.

If we are all one family, then we must think and act for the welfare of the other members. More than just money is needed; people need to have control of their own lives and need to have solidarity in their struggles. Finding solutions to global problems needs commitment to social justice.

We practise loving kindness

An interview with Dr. A. T. Ariyaratna
Bristol, England

I first heard about Dr. A. T. Ariyaratna in 1980 when someone said to me, 'Have you met the Gandhi of Sri Lanka, a man named Dr. Ariyaratna? He is the founder of probably the largest self-help project for villages to be found in the world.' I hadn't. It was four years later in Bristol that I met him. I listened to him give the annual Schumacher Society lecture and met with him the following day in his hotel room, during which time I learnt about his tireless work in the villages of Sri Lanka.

In 1958 Dr Ariyaratna, a young science teacher at Nalanda College, a Buddhist high school in the capital of Colombo, organized a two-week holiday work camp for a group of 16- and 17-year-old students in a remote and poverty-stricken village. They called the camp *shramadana* (from *shrama*, which means labour, or human energy, and *dana* which means to give). It was not long before numerous other schools on the island began supporting weekend village camps.

Dr Ariyaratna then went to India to spend time with and learn from Vinoba Bhave, who was walking around India campaigning for the return of land to the villages from the wealthy landlords. When he returned to Sri Lanka, he decided to adopt the name under which co-workers could initiate projects in the village and uplift village life – the Sarvodaya Shramadana Movement. Sarvodaya, a word used by Gandhi, means 'awakening for all'. In the past twenty years tens of thousands of workers have been able to participate in massive village self-help projects, involving health, education, agriculture, village industry, the arts and the application of Buddhist values.

There is no doubt that Dr Ariyaratna is a tireless worker in the villages of Sri Lanka. In February, 1986 I visited Sri Lanka on behalf of the Buddhist Peace Fellowship. Accompanied by David

Arnott, founder of the BPF in Britain, we visited Dr Ariyaratna at his headquarters and training centre in Moratuwa just outside Colombo.

We stayed with him and his family in their home at the center. On the evening of our arrival we listened to him talk to more than 1000 young workers who had come to the centre from countless villages for meetings and workshops. Dr Ariyaratna, or Ari as he is referred to affectionately, exudes the air of a man with a mission who won't waver or falter until his last breath of life.

In my observation of him in the brief spell at Moratuwa, he had the appearance of someone who was extending himself beyond reason. There were a seemingly endless stream of visitors, including overseas aid workers, Sarvodaya organizers and villagers with problems who came and went.

He is a warm affectionate human being with a genuine spirit of loving kindness which seems to have a joyful impact on the Sarvodaya workers. And although Ari was very keen to show me his tiny meditation room in his home, I had the distinct feeling that he was under some stress due to this unflagging commitment to others.

Apart from a long and utterly demanding day, he has the added pressure of responsibility without any government sponsorship. The conflict and violence existing between the Sinhalese government and the Tamils demanding an independent state on the island was obviously deeply troubling Ari as well. His appeals and efforts for a peaceful solution were being totally ignored despite his immense popularity throughout the island. His hopes for a resolution satisfying to Sinhalese and Tamils alike were being dashed by the day. So I left wondering whether or not Ari was not just throwing himself more and more into the Sarvodaya movement as a way of avoiding the complexity of the political violence that was engulfing parts of this green and beautiful island. A small number of his workers had been killed or injured in the armed conflict, too.

As the work of the Sarvodaya movement has gained international attention it has meant that more and more money has been donated from overseas, especially Holland, Germany and the US. What this means is that the organization has to integrate the philosophy of self-reliance with overseas support. Success brings its own difficulties.

Certainly a major foundation of the self-help movement in the world today embraces several of the basic themes of Theravada

Buddhism, including the Noble Eightfold Path, meditation, the application of loving kindness and compassion and the significance of awakening. During the course of the interview Ari gladly touched on these themes which are clearly inseparable from the task of mobilizing popular participation in all aspects of village life for the welfare of all.

CT: The first question which I would like to ask about is the use of the word *sarvodaya*. You translate this as 'awakening for all'. Awakening to what?

A: I would say, awakening to reality. For each human being awakening is different at different times. For a person who hasn't got the basic needs of life, his awakening will be, first, to work hard to get food to feed his family. Then gradually the person begins to look within himself or herself and tries to discover how one could be happier. According to the Buddhist philosophy, in order to be happy we must be less greedy, less violent and less ignorant. We have to cultivate the opposite qualities: not greed but sharing, not violence but love, not ignorance but enlightenment. So the word 'awakening' embraces all this. For practical purposes, we see awakening as our objective.

CT: When you are working with people in the villages, is inner awakening actually emphasized?

A: We emphasize it fully, not partly. We say inner awakening is the crux of what we are doing. For example, we had to construct a building. That is a very important physical job to be done. Constructing a building is useless if it is done without cultivating other qualities. We say that those who are working on the project are 'gifting' their labour; not only those who are getting benefit from this work but outsiders who may never come again to this place. We believe in oneness and kindness for all. That is the first quality. When we work we share our thoughts, feelings, our effort with others, we don't expect anything in return. We practise loving kindness; we apply compassionate action and when we do it as a spiritual endeavour, we feel joy immediately, a dispassionate joy. When we work like that people may laugh at us; some people may abuse us; some may curse us. So we look at ourselves very closely and develop equanimity. These four qualities – kindness, compassion, joy and equanimity — are kept in mind for personal awakening.

CT: In the West, conscious people are often either totally externalized, doing for others, or they are internalized, working on themselves. In the villages, how do you bring the outer and inner together?

A: Every activity we do in the village begins with a few minutes of meditation and loving kindness. This brings a certain spiritual unity and inner communication. In order to bring a spiritual unity, we do not make any decisions by taking a majority vote. Everything is decided by consensus. We do not allow any consideration of politics to come into our work.

CT: How have you resisted that? Generally as small grass roots organizations get bigger the tendency is to become *more* political and *more* centralized.

A: Our principle is decentralization by not trying to acquire more power. We believe the concentration of power, whether political or economic, is the root cause of the chaotic situation in the world. We believe in a very strong decentralization of power. In other words, we don't need people wielding power. We can work together in the village if we have a strong moral and spiritual foundation. We find that hard work along with song and dance helps to build this foundation. Music has a great impact on day-to-day thinking in the life of the people. We compose our own songs, dances and dramas where the higher moral and spiritual values are emphasized.

CT: The Buddha frequently emphasized the interdependence of life and compassionate action for people, creatures and environment as well as such elements as meditation and right livelihood. In the West, we don't have this kind of philosophical and spiritual foundation. How can we explore this way of living?

A: First, the need must be recognized. There are many people in the West who have realized that something is fundamentally missing. Material needs are already largely satisfied. Then people begin to realize that a materialistic consumer-orientated sort of life is meaningless. So perhaps communication can be established between people who are wanting to live with a spiritual foundation.

In our villages we have a communication process set up where families correspond with other families in other parts of the world.

They send art, stories and songs in addition to letters. We ask a child to write a letter to another child describing what they do and ask them to reply to what's happening in their community. Though it looks very simple, this sort of thing immediately makes both children realize they are living in one world and they have a lot of important things in common in their present situation and in their future which they can share.

We have communicated with the world in this way. There are some 120 communities in Sri Lanka that communicate with villages in England, the US and other countries. We talk so much about meditation so our overseas friends naturally become interested. They ask, 'What is meditation? Just closing our eyes and sitting in a place? Why does it have meaning?' Something happens without our knowledge while we are meditating. We are not only bringing about a sensory level of communication but a certain, I should say, super sensory level of communication.

CT: I'm not sure I understand.

A: The build-up of consciousness is cumulative. When there are a number of people feeling the same way then there is a certain force created. It is unbelievable yet it is so infectious! Supposing 100 of us lived here together and followed a single vision, like believing in the oneness of the living world or in simplicity of life. This would create a certain psychological or thought sphere which could influence a community of people even though they knew nothing at all about it. They would start thinking about the same things. In the same way that polluted air can bring about disease, an unpolluted thought sphere can remove a lot of polluted thinking in the world.

In the world today there is so much interest in Buddhist philosophy and practice. People are trying to relate it to their lives and to their development. What is important is for somebody to start now. In the West sometimes I don't mention the word 'Buddhism' because I don't want people to think that I have come to propagate a particular religion. I prefer to express freely Buddhist thoughts in action.

CT: In the West, we may have sufficient material goods for ourselves but many of us lack awareness of the interrelatedness of life. So through correspondence, interaction, meditative practices and togetherness we can establish unity. What else do we need to be more aware of?

A: I believe you should start a very broad form of sharing. In Holland, for example, there is a tradition: Before a meal is taken an extra plate is put on the table as a reminder that while you enjoy your food, there are those who do not have food. The youngest child can put a handful of rice or coins onto the plate and that is an offering for anybody in need here or somewhere else.

Last night we saw this film on Ethiopia. The film reminds us not to waste and not to indulge in pleasure of the senses. The Buddha taught us the Middle Way. If people live in extremes they will feel a lot of suffering in the body. There are certain religious people who inflict a lot of pain to their body through self-denial. It's not the way to discover truth. When the Buddha referred to people who satisfy their senses without limit, like what is happening in the West, he said, 'This is vulgar.' He said if you want to discover the truth, first, take what is necessary for your body so that your mind can function properly, and *then* look for the truth.

CT: The West is gradually becoming more aware of the wisdom of the East through meditation, yoga, T'ai Chi, healing, medicine and through the example of people like Gandhi, Vinobe Bhave, yourself and others who are applying the principles of spirituality to very difficult external situations. This is a very important message for our Western setting. There is real interest to make bridges between spiritual and social reality.

A: If someone is not making the bridge, a person might be doing good for an anti-nuclear campaign, for example, but he or she may neglect their inner life. Someone who does ecological work may be involved in another trade which is not in accord with ecological awareness. He or she could be making a lot of money out of it in a very unjust way. It is not enough to campaign on one issue; it is important to integrate other disciplines as well, like meditation. These problems are interrelated and the interrelationship should be expressed in action.

CT: In England there is an ongoing debate between people in the Green movement who say we should not be concerned with gaining political power and those in the Green Party who say we should use every endeavour to gain political representation at any level. What is your view on this?

A: If you start from a grass roots organization, there is a difference between that party and other parties to begin with. But if you just want a party for the sake of capturing power, what are you going to capture? You are going to capture a certain instrument which was not only used by other people to create these problems but the instrument is a problem itself.

CT: Could you clarify?

A: The British Parliament is said to function as the best in the world. We thought we could use it in our countries but we couldn't. Only when a certain material, educational and intellectual level of development is reached in a society can you use a party system. When you take a system from one society and try to fit it into another society, there is a lot of exploitation and inequality. That's why I said the root cause of most of our problems in our societies is the party system, where greed for power is organized. I advocate work at the grass roots level. We need organizations right across the country where no dictator, no elected leader can disturb it.

CT: I do feel that the Green movement and the spiritual movement is still rather fragmented with too little sense of interconnectedness. What way can we work at the grass roots level to establish this connectedness?

A: I think you don't have to worry too much about that, as long as the groups don't compete with each other. For example, there was no rain for a long time here but then as the rains came many little streams of water began to flow. As time went on the wetter streams began to join and revitalize the river. It's like that now. Various people in Sri Lanka ask me this same question. I tell them, 'Don't worry, go ahead with what you can according to the sacrifice you can make. Go ahead.' All these things are coming together.

People are going to realize the interrelatedness between greed and environmental destruction, between greed for power and nuclear weapons. We don't want a party society. We make sacrifices and we share. Your community can belong to our community so immediately we have a universal perspective. One movement becomes connected with another movement in another country. You can't just forget your neighbour. We are all linked.

CT: You said, 'It's fine as long as they are not competitive,' but we are an extremely competitive society.

A: One person who is in a situation where a lot of competitiveness prevails can develop an inner mental power. Every morning and evening he or she can think, 'May the entire world live together and be happy.' If an individual or a group does this it is only a matter of time before all the others will get drawn in. Meditation should be like this. When you stand on this bank and see water flowing between your bank and another bank you think there is no connection between the two. Actually the two banks are linked by groundwater. Draw as many people as possible together for meditation. Don't talk. Meditate. This may be the connecting force, which is the only force that can undo that competitiveness and win co-operation.

CT: You've mentioned the value and importance of children connecting with each other as well as adults. What would be the process of other grass roots movements and individuals to make contact with Sarvodaya?

A: We ask people to write to our special division called 'the village link-up programme'. They will write back and suggest a name of a village to make contact with. There are many rich groups who want to help the poor, and yet real co-operation and inter-connectedness is not possible without co-sharing. The rich group sees that a community with say, about 50 pre-school children who don't get proper nutrition need 350 rupees (£10) for food. Surely this community can easily provide that for the other community. In return the poor community would send 10 stories emphasizing Buddhist values. So that is not gain. It's sharing.

CT: What is your position in Sarvodaya?

A: I'm the president, but I want my name to be out of the movement and for it to go on so that I do not dabble in administration too much. Of course, I have power and authority there but I don't abuse it. There are seventy-five members in the executive council and seventeen in the officials committee who manage the day-to-day affairs of the administration. I devote my time to meeting with different groups around the world where Sarvodaya is working and to different projects, like in Africa where I visit our volunteers who are working there. Then when I come back I'll be continuously working for maybe three or four months before I decide to go out again for a week or two. But most of the time I spend in the villages.

CT: If a person says, 'I wish to do something,' where would she or he start?'

A: I would first say, if that person gets up at 6.00 a.m. every morning, get up at 5.45 a.m. instead. Begin the morning by sitting down with the body erect, adopt a nice posture, right hand on left hand and observe the body from head to foot and from toes to the head. Relax every muscle. With the mind you look at the body. This is to understand the mind–body relationship. Then practise the breathing exercise, mindfulness of breathing in and breathing out. This is to conserve energy. Then practise loving kindness, thinking of one's body being healthy, thinking of one's mind being healthy by having less greed, hatred and ignorance. Then focus on one's parents, children, husband, wife, family and all humanity. May the world be happy. This is the spiritual preparation. Look at your loved ones with compassion.

When you practise every day like that you will see lots of things to do in your immediate surroundings. You will begin to realize that every word you speak, every action you take is in relationship to your own personality. Awakening must be your fulfilment. Then according to your ability you can make other sacrifices. By way of monetary actions you can help the community within the country or outside your country by sharing what you have justly earned or inherited to make other people happy. Then it becomes a self-generating process.

Anybody can start this way. I own no land, no property. I earn no income. I've had nobody to look after me my whole life. I have children but we have nothing to call our own. What other people have given us we have given back to the movement. So you can do a tremendous amount of work and you don't lose anything. I don't think many people get the love and hospitality that I enjoy around the world and yet I don't have anything to call mine.

CT: So money comes in and one can continue. It requires a certain faith. Giving of oneself even in small ways is the spiritual tradition.

A: Yes, I agree.

PSYCHOLOGY OF CHANGE

The new paradigm

An interview with Fritjof Capra
Berkeley, California

When Fritjof Capra brought out his book *The Tao of Physics*, it represented a milestone in the analysis of some of the religious and philosophical insights of the East as related to contemporary Western science and physics. Since the book was first published in 1976, it has become an international best seller in its field. Nearly three quarters of a million copies have been sold and it has been translated into a dozen languages.

Fritjof was born and educated in Austria where, in 1966, he received his Ph.D. in physics at the University of Vienna. From there he moved to France, where he researched theoretical high-energy physics at the University of Paris.

In 1969, while sitting by the ocean late one summer afternoon, he experienced 'the whole environment as being engaged in a gigantic cosmic dance'. There was a sudden realization that the mind of the scientist and the mind of the mystic were not so far apart as one would think. Further, Capra had also been attracted to Zen Buddhism, where the meditative inquiry into the paradox and puzzles of quantum theory bore a marked resemblance. Not surprisingly, he dedicated his first book to such people as Krishnamurti, Alan Watts and Carlos Castenada.

The next step took him to California, where there is a vast array of exploration taking place in various fields, including philosophy, cosmology, astronomy, physics, psychotherapy, Eastern thought, the religious experience and mysticism. The exposure to all this made its impact on the mind and consciousness of Fritjof. As he went about his research, he began to see again and again a direct correlation between the exploration of the scientist employing experimentation and hypothesis, with the exploration of the meditator employing inner observation with spiritual disciplines.

Capra recalls how a spiritual insight emerged from the depths of his consciousness without any effort or planning. 'Coming, as it did, after years of detailed analytical thinking, it was so overwhelming that I burst into tears.'

Although he is not a political organizer, he is an avid speaker for the international Green movement. With Charlene Spretnak, he co-authored *Green Politics*, an analysis of the contemporary state of the Green movement. It was the winner of the New Options Political Book Award for 1985.

Fritjof presently lives in the Elmwood district of Berkeley, California with his wife and child. Apart from being on the faculty at the University of California, he is also a founder and director of the Elmwood Institute, named after the district in which he lives. The purpose of the institute is to create an intellectual resource base for the Green movement, which Capra says is still in its formative years. The institute organizes seminars for the exploration of green concerns and publishes a newsletter.

It might be appropriate to describe Fritjof as an intellectual visionary. He fulfils an intensely valuable role in the green movement by pointing out to the scientific, academic and business communities, the failings, if not destructiveness, of old ways of thinking which fragment life into mind, body and environment. In his latest book, *The Turning Point*, he says that this mechanistic view is an outdated perception. Both physics and spirituality share similar holistic and ecological perceptions from a viewpoint of totality rather than separation.

One of Fritjof's major contributions is that he is able to speak and write to an influential and privileged group of intellectuals within Western society and thus to some extent, act as a spokesperson for many grass roots activists who simply do not have access to that vast repertoire of scientific and biological concepts. To some extent, he is acting as a bridge between two seemingly polarized perceptions.

At the time of the interview he was clearly switching his focus from writing as a primary activity to directly communicating with people through public talks and seminars, especially with the business, political and scientific communities. He is also interfacing with the green movement.

CT: Could you briefly summarize your book *The Turning Point?*

FC: I think it is the first book that offers a grand synthesis for an emerging new vision of reality, an emerging new paradigm that includes concepts, perceptions, values and modes of action. I recently had the thought that it may also be the last book of its kind. Parts of this emerging new vision were described in other books, including my first book, *The Tao of Physics. The Turning Point* provides an overall grand vision. It has now got to the point where so many people are working on various aspects of this vision with so many new ideas that a summary is no longer possible.

CT: In your books you incorporate perceptions and consciousness and the way that this affects our whole way of living and being. Since the publication of your book what steps have you taken to explore ways to implement these awarenesses?

FC: The implementation is my main work now. I am not working on any further elaboration of theoretical concepts, although I have a very theoretical mind. Naturally when I give seminars I have new ideas and I write articles about them. Here at UC Berkeley I teach a course about ecology and peace which I call 'Deep ecology – the paradigm of peace.' I give lots of lectures and seminars around the country. I also speak to business people, to corporate executives and managers to show them how new perceptions can be applied in the management of business and economics.

Three years ago I founded an institute called the 'Elmwood Institute', after this area where we live. The institute's purpose is to serve as a bridge between ideas and action. I have come to believe that this change of consciousness could and should happen much faster if we want to avoid catastrophe.

CT: So you are moving away from being a writer to more direct, personal communication.

FC: Yes. This is not an abrupt change. When I wrote *The Turning Point* I had a group of advisors. These people wrote background papers for me and I also had many discussions with them. It was a collaborative effort, although I wrote the book entirely alone. I'm also very inspired by the people who attend my seminars, so I get a lot of material from other people. The starting point is the recognition that the major problems of our time are all part and parcel of the same crisis – a crisis of perception. By major problems I mean the threat of nuclear war, the devastation of the natural environment, the persistence of hunger and poverty around the world. Our social institutions, our politicians, business people and so on are using an outdated world view to solve these problems, a world view which is no longer appropriate. At the same time we are seeing a change of consciousness, an emerging new vision of reality. I describe to them this new vision as it emerges in science and in the various social movements: the ecology movement, the peace movement, the women's movement, spiritual movement and so on.

CT: Could you say a little more about this outdated world view?

FC: Our dominant culture is in its decline because it subscribes to outdated concepts and values. In a declining culture people feel that things don't work the way they used to, so instead of changing they go back even further to old values. The force of this conservative backlash has been stronger than I thought, although Arnold Toynbee and other cultural historians predicted it. The situation is now more critical. The conservative forces are stronger and the alternative forces are stronger. So it becomes important to promote non-violence explicitly as an essential aspect of the new paradigm.

CT: There is also a noticeable marriage of the conservative forces with orthodox, fundamentalist religion.

FC: The cultural transformation is of such a depth that it cuts through all the fields. So you have the same paradigm shift and conservative backlash in religion. You'll also find this backlash in science. Just think of all the scientists who work for the military. It is difficult to tell if the backlash is gaining momentum. It's hard to make predictions with regard to cultural change. We don't really have a theory of social change.

CT: The alternatives or complementary movements are in the ascendant?

FC: Yes, without any doubt. Let me give you an example. Daniel Ellsberg told me that the Democrats commissioned a series of secret public opinion polls to work out an election strategy. They found that the American people nationwide are very scared about anything nuclear – nuclear tests, nuclear bombs, nuclear waste, nuclear energy, you name it. The media here systematically tried to eliminate the debate about nuclear power after Chernobyl. They sent out the message that this could never happen here. But public opinion went in the opposite direction and people spoke out. What seems like a conservative dominating force may be very shallow. Underneath people get more and more ready for change. So for us who work on new visions and new political ways this is very important. For example, Christopher, you are not going to be elected when you run for Parliament in Britain as a Green Party candidate so you have an excellent chance of not compromising and of really telling people the way things are.

CT: Peace, ecology, the women's movement, the influence of Eastern philosophy, the alternatives in medicine, education, science, and technology, the development of psychotherapy – they are all making inroads. At the same time, one also sees a remarkable resistance to change. The media frequently have a critical, if not negative view towards anything that is a step away from the status quo.

FC: This is absolutely true. Speaking for the American situation, the media are owned by industry, as are politicians. Industry and business – the corporate community – have heavily invested in the status quo. They don't want to change it. The media condition people to an incredible extent. However, there are also alternative journals, newsletters, radio stations and other kinds of programmes available.

CT: Concepts and language are, as you pointed out in your books, extremely influential on people's psyche. Just take one concept, *non-violence*, as an example. As important and essential as it is, I think it awakens in too many minds a feeling of being passive, withdrawn and fearful. There are millions of voices supporting violence at many levels. I think that what is often forgotten is that non-violence is to be equated with sustained communication at all costs.

FC: Yes, that's very well put. As we know from Gandhi, non-violence is not at all passive. This knowledge is now re-expressed and re-kindled in the politics of the green movement. The greens are clearly non-violent and have this explicitly in their principles.

CT: Owing to the rapidity of change, concepts get quickly outmoded.

FC: They change faster because the world becomes evermore interconnected with the modern means of communication. It doesn't take so long for a development in one part of the world to be known in another part.

CT: In England we have a reasonably coherent philosophy in the Green Party manifesto, including such themes as non-violence, ecological awareness and grass roots democracy. In the US one feels a tremendous diversity of grass roots activity but at the same time, it remains individualistic.

FC: That's right. The green movement is coming together slower because the country is much larger. If you look at the history of the green movement in Germany you see it begins in cities. The cities there are not far from each other, so things go on locally. Here in the Bay Area there is a group called the East Bay Greens, there is the San Francisco Greens, the North Coast Greens and the South Coast Greens and often these groups know little about each other. On the other hand, it is no use at this point having a national organization and a candidate for president. Nothing will change in American politics. We have to be really clear of our purpose. I'm not a political organizer; I'm in communication with the green movement. I created the Elmwood Institute explicitly for the purpose of providing an intellectual resource base for the green movement.

CT: In England there is certainly a lack of adequate global analysis, even though the Conservative and Labour parties have decades of research to draw upon. To what degree is there sufficient reflection, analysis and publication taking place in green movement?

FC: Not much in the green movement because the organization is just beginning, but people are meeting. For instance, we had a symposium of some thirty presenters and critics of the new paradigm who met together in a secluded place for five days. We explored a lot of different areas and asked a lot of questions. For example: is the term 'paradigm' useful at all? Where is the serious research? What are the inconsistencies? What needs to be synthesized? What is the state of the European movements?

CT: What about the spiritual element within green issues? How does it compare to the European movements?

FC: It is much stronger here than in Europe. Ecological awareness is at the very centre of green politics. At its deepest level this is also spiritual awareness, because ecological awareness recognizes the fundamental interconnectedness of everything. We are embedded in the cosmos as individuals and as societies. In this country the green movement recognizes that explicitly and therefore tries to incorporate the spiritual into the political right from the start.

CT: I agree. I experience a sense of receptivity and interest when one touches on our spiritual relationship to people, creatures and environment. From your point of view, what happened in Europe?

FC: Being European I travel back and forth all the time and so get a pretty clear picture. The new awareness is emerging on both sides of the Atlantic but it takes very different forms. In California during the seventies, you had the so-called New Age movement – the occult, humanistic psychology and holistic health care – which was heavily orientated towards spirituality. There was a noticeable lack of political awareness and social consciousness. This phase is over now. In Europe throughout the seventies, the alternative movements were still drawing their energies from the student movements of 1968 and were heavily politically orientated. Many had a Marxist or new left background. They were much more politically astute, but on the other side they had very little notion of what it was to live a healthy life. They managed stress very badly. There was also a noticeable lack of connection with spiritual values.

CT: Why?

FC: In Germany the combination of spirituality and politics has a Nazi flavour so it was to be avoided at all costs. Now the situation is slowly changing on both sides. Californians are becoming more astute politically and the Europeans are becoming more spiritual and healthier. This moving together is helped because a lot of interchange is taking place.

CT: Greens from Europe certainly come here to the US but what about green activists going from here to Europe?

FC: The Europeans sometimes feel they can't learn much from the Americans so they don't invite them. The Americans can't go on their own because they don't have the money. The German greens, comparatively, have a lot of money because they make money with every election. They run very cheap campaigns and then they get large refunds from the State so they send people over here on fact-finding tours.

CT: I'd like to shift to the personal level, especially since your daughter was born recently. One of the difficulties we are faced with is how to integrate our global concerns wth our personal responsibilities as a parent and partner.

FC: Well, I've just gone through a phase in my life which was very important. My daughter, Juliette, is now eight months old. She was born right here in this room. I spent the first three months entirely at home, not attending to my usual work at all. She has two parents who mother and nurture her. I think this last point is extremely important, not only for the children but also for the parents and especially for men.

During the first few days I experienced a tremendous appreciation for women. When you have a newborn infant you can't get anything together. Breakfast before noon? Forget it! It is such an emotional, mental and physical change. Every two hours you get up. Just imagine that women traditionally did this alone and then not just with one baby but two or more. Other women were involved and supporting, but now with nuclear families many women have been doing it alone.

A baby becomes a connecting point with anybody. When you have a baby with you, you can connect with people at the purely human level. Race, religion, male, female, age – none of that seems to matter. For me I'm very eager to have intellectual discussions, organize them and write about them. But now anybody with a baby is so much more interesting than anybody else. So I really believe that if men got involved with that intensity we certainly wouldn't need a women's movement. And, of course, it would be better for society as a whole.

CT: In that respect a young life is a factor showing our interconnectedness with each other.

FC: We learn a lot, too. [Fritjof is holding the baby in his arms and says to the baby, 'We have been talking about you.'] She is still at the stage where she thinks, 'He who speaks does not know and she who knows does not speak.'

CT: Now that your daughter is eight months old you focus around the parenting role?

FC: Yes. We worked out a schedule where I get up around seven in the morning. From seven until ten I am at home and will help my wife take care of the baby and spend time with her. From about 10 a.m. to 1 p.m. I write. In the afternoon I have her for about half the time. Just before you came I was working in my office and she was crawling around on the floor, so the work is really shared.

CT: As you expressed earlier, the present model of the nuclear family is under incredible threat. There is not the support of the old system.

FC: The nuclear family is a very clever invention of the business world because it maximizes consumption. Each family has a vacuum cleaner and a toaster and a car, or even two cars, and all the other gadgets that came out especially during the fifties with all that technological optimism. If you want to see it cynically and in an exaggerated way, in order to maximize consumption, they put people in little concrete blocks. In the sixties, there was a reaction to all of this with the starting of the communes. The communes didn't work very well. They were not supported by the surrounding society, although a few of them did quite well and are still functioning. There is much to be done at the local level.

CT: Thank you for including your personal and social life along with your ecological awareness in this interview. Thank you, Juliette, for listening and being so patient.

FC: She will now eat the microphone to conclude the interview!

The liberation of women

An interview with Christina Feldman
Totnes, Devon, England

I first met Christina Feldman in Dharamsala, Himachel Pradesh, India, in the foothills of the Himalayas in 1974. She was 22 years old, married and engaged full time in the study and practice of Mahayana Buddhism. Her spiritual journey took her to India from Canada when she was 17 years old.

And, as she recalls, she found herself looking outwardly to authority and tradition for the answers she was seeking. Living in Dharamsala she was exposed to the Tibetan teachings and was one of the first students of the respected teacher, Geshe Rabten.

She also participated in a number of ten-day intensive meditation retreats with teachers, including myself, who were influenced by the Theravada Buddhist tradition. These retreats emphasize sustained mindfulness meditation when sitting, walking, standing and eating. The day begins at 4.30 a.m. and finishes with a hot drink at 9.30 p.m. The retreats employing vipassana (insight) meditation give the opportunity for a person to make deep contact with themselves in the total silence of the environment from moment to moment both at the psychological level as well as giving access to deep religious experiences.

In 1975 I was living in Dalhousie for five months conducting retreats in some old large rented houses in that part of the Himalayan foothills. Some 60 people were participating in the programme, including Christina. Not many weeks went by before people there began to recognize that Christina had much to offer in the way of insights and understanding of the human condition.

Since that time she has facilitated retreats throughout the world, working with other teachers, including myself, and by herself. Her quiet, unblemished matter-of-fact talks are given to groups of up to 100 people from all walks of life. More than 100 of her talks are on tape.

Born in Yorkshire in 1952, she spent the first five years of her life in England until her parents emigrated to Canada. She returned to live in England in May, 1977. In September of that year, she co-founded (with myself) the Gilletts Community in Smarden, Kent, where twenty of us lived in a large eleven-bedroomed house.

Now married to Mick Rusling, a social worker, she has two children, Sara, aged eight years and Aaron, aged five years. In 1983, she moved from Gilletts to Totnes, Devon where she co-founded Gaia House, an international retreat centre. She is a member of the international board of the Buddhist Peace Fellowship.

In recent years Christina has expanded the forms of her retreats to include retreats for families and for women. Voices of appreciation and gratitude have come from women of all backgrounds, ages and persuasions who have participated in her retreats.

Christina says that we have to be willing to risk the loss of external dependency, affirmation and approval if we are to know ourselves deeply. She says that the 'validity of our spirituality can only be qualified by our own experience and understanding. Through meditation we can untangle the conditioning that leads us to prostrate ourselves before authority.'

Such words strike a chord with many concerned women not only with regard to spiritual authority but other forms of external authority. Despite Christina's reflections and inquiry into the vast field of spiritual awareness, she continues to make it clear to women and men that she does not want to be perceived as some kind of authority in this or other areas.

As well as being a retreat leader, parent, householder and workshop facilitator, she has also managed to find time to write a book called *Woman Awake* (Penguin Books). The book is an inquiry into and a celebration of women's spirituality.

The interview with Christina explores contemporary issues facing women.

CT: At the present time, we are experiencing a noticeable and significant change in the consciousness of women as they discover in fresh ways the sense of their authority. How can a woman guard against imitating some of the ways in which men have used and abused power? Typical examples are the male domination in politics, religion, the legal profession and the workplace.

CF: As women become increasingly conscious of themselves, they become correspondingly aware of the dynamic of power. Women also see the negative conditioning they carry. Part of women's conditioning is to believe that the real power centres exist primarily outside of themselves. These outside power centres have the authority to dispense values, models, and rules that govern our appearance, presentation, direction and goals. These centres also dispense approval and disapproval, acceptability and unacceptability. Part of most women's conditioning is to believe these powers are somewhat infallible.

CT: What is the effect of this belief?

CF: The destructive effect of this is that women begin pursuing models of how they think they should be in order to be acceptable, feel worthy and appear feminine. To follow that way of living is basically a way of disempowering ourselves because there is a constant looking for credentials to see whether we have succeeded or failed in conforming to these models.

CT: So the negative conditioning for a woman is to place authority and power outside of herself.

CF: Yes, so the final arbiter of worthiness is placed in anything that's perceived to have authority – institutions, social values, traditions or beliefs. Anything can seem to have the power to dispense acceptability.

CT: Are women choosing to place this power outwardly?

CF: It's not a conscious choice. It is a collusion between women and those who are either set up or set themselves up as authorities. It's an unconscious choice. It is rooted in not knowing any source of inner empowerment. Women don't necessarily acknowledge this as long as they are alienated from a source of inner empowerment.

Also, these power centres exist only as long as they are believed in. For example, the Church may say women cannot become priests. If that power centre is not believed in then those dictates fall in a vacuum. Buddhist monks may say that women can't have equal ordination. If that power isn't given to the monks then the dictate doesn't have any meaning.

CT: A woman may say, 'Yes, I keep transferring this power to these voices of authority. I can't stop myself from doing it. I just

don't seem to believe in myself, in my gender. What can I do?'
What would you say?

CF: The first step is to be really conscious that she is actually
doing that, that she is actually giving her power away. The first
step of being conscious is also the first step in bringing about
change. What follows from that is to find support for such a change
so there comes about the courage to question how infallible these
power centres are.

CT: How would you define 'power' in this context?

CF: I define 'power' as an energy that holds the capacity to transform or change. It's neither negative nor positive. It is an energy that
everyone has within themselves. What we are primarily exposed to
in our life is a degeneration of power. Negative power is frequently
backed by motives of fear and insecurity and the taking up of fixed
positions.

   Often within institutions, the powers that be are very unwilling
to change. They don't wish to give up their power base at all or
their role in that power base. If it is unacceptable, a woman has to
step out of it. In one sense, to resist a negative power structure
gives as much power to it as to subscribe to it. The power structure
still supports the belief that they exist as a power centre and is
worthy of obedience or resistance. I am saying this on the basis
that the particular institution in question is unwilling to change.
Power centres have, of course, an investment in being a power
centre. They don't want to lose that, otherwise they would stop
being a power centre. The investment is propped up by unfathom-
able depths of insecurity and fear. So any changes will initially
bring about a lot of resistance.

CT: What else is important to bring about change?

CF: It's also important for women to look for radically new
sources of power and new ways of using power, otherwise women
will also begin to operate power centres in the same way – supported basically by fear and insecurity. This means that no real
change has taken place. If women can discover sources of power
within themselves, a pure power, then the power will be rooted in
wisdom, rooted in inner trust. This power is not caught up in a
struggle between for and against, or a struggle to convert or

manipulate. Women who are rooted in trust and wisdom will simply be saying that this is what we understand to be true.

CT: And if there is still an unwillingness to be heard?

CF: Then the ingredients for change are simply not there. One way that women can offer change is by using power in a qualitatively different way – by offering clear alternatives.

CT: But isn't sustained resistance to the status quo a valid activity?

CF: Yes, it is. For example, I find myself rubbing up against traditional Buddhists. I know that Theravada Buddhism [one of the main Buddhist traditions] isn't going to change overnight, if at all, in its attitude towards women's ordination. The rules don't allow it. I don't say, 'Well, forget it. I'm not going to deal with you guys.' It simply means that I am going to go on speaking the truth as I see it. I hope somewhere it will touch someone and encourage them to question. That doesn't mean to say I wouldn't explore a viable alternative. I don't feel bound to the inequalities the tradition may uphold, therefore I can draw upon the richness of the tradition without in any way being limited by it.

CT: What sort of things do you have in mind when you say 'viable alternatives' and 'fresh ways of working and moving out of old models?'

CF: For example, participating in women's retreats. Women's retreats create an environment in which women do not have to keep proving themselves. It is a way of empowering women inwardly. The environment creates a trust which is conducive to developing inner trust. Out of that environment women leave connected with inner sources of power which, perhaps, they haven't connected with before. They don't feel devalued just because they are women. Out of this, networks of conscious women can be formed. Perhaps, for certain women, one day will come when there is an ordained religious order that has not sought permission of the monks to be ordained.

CT: Isn't there the possibility, though, of women becoming increasingly separatist in their world view?

CF: The emphasis which I give in working with women safeguards against that. Separatism comes out of blaming men. I'm not interested in placing blame. I emphasize very much not wasting energy by consuming ourselves or even concerning ourselves with blame. That places the source and cause of the problem totally with external factors.

CT: Which is to make it a power centre.

CF: Yes. Of course. I emphasize that a way of evading participation in that destructive power system is by displacing the responsibility for it, by saying it is *all* outside of oneself. We easily see structures and power centres as adversaries forgetting that adversaries are given that role by the presence of a victim. On one level, men seem to benefit from the power systems that exist, but essentially everybody loses. Division is detrimental to everyone's well-being. I make that very clear.

CT: In what ways are men losing out?

CF: Any power structure which resists challenge and questioning rests so much on fear, and this breeds tightness, narrowness of vision and inner alienation. Clinging to power prevents men from an open and receptive way of being, from receiving the feminine within themselves. Such people have to concern themselves constantly with protection, defence and aggression in order to keep others from participating.

CT: That's a grave situation.

CF: Right. Let me add further to the issue of separatism. Women's retreats and workshops do not exist as opposite to mixed retreats or male retreats. That's not the purpose of them at all. It is basically to provide a particular kind of environment which emphasizes the maximum degree of ease in communication and inner exploration. For many women that happens primarily in a single sex environment, at least at some point in their lives. It is also not separatist because it is not an attempt to create another kind of institution with a leader, hierarchy and belief system. And that is very important.

CT: What do women experience with each other?

CF: Women learn the fundamental response of opening and not closing off to anything; they learn that women have much to offer to each other and bring a balance to the feminine and masculine dynamic. We do not promote the feminine as being superior but seek to find an inner rapport between the feminine and masculine within. I don't use those concepts as being purely gender-orientated.

They can be evocative concepts. For example, receptivity is usually regarded as a feminine quality but action is regarded as masculine; pliability is regarded as feminine and discipline as masculine; emotion as feminine and intellect as masculine. Everyone holds within themselves all of those qualities but our conditioning leads us to emphasize one over the other. This often is in detriment to our own balance.

CT: Is wholeness an integration of the feminine and masculine qualities?

CF: Wholeness is a mutual rapport, a co-operative relationship between the variety of dynamics.

CT: There is also a diversity of perceptions and values among women about their place in the world. Women have traditional and conservative views with the centrality of their role being focused around the home as a mother and wife.

CF: There's nothing wrong with those roles. I think we must find our place in the world in which we feel free and fulfilled. When roles are adopted out of insecurity or conditioning, they become not roles but reality. Then it is impossible to grow. 'I am a mother and that's all that I am.' 'I am a wife and that is all I ever will be.'

When someone assumes a conclusion about one's identity it safeguards against the insecurity that arises in exploring freedom. We may feel insecure when we challenge our realities and begin to expand beyond the roles. So out of insecurity we hold on to our stated reality.

CT: In other words, if one identifies with a role, one is inhibiting oneself.

CF: You limit your sense of possibility.

CT: Some women will say, 'Look, I haven't got any choice. I am house-bound and role-bound. I don't have time or money to go on retreats and workshops or to grow with other women.' How would you respond to that?

CF: The physical environment for the role doesn't determine if one is bound. Some women will feel incredibly bound by the role and other women in the same environment will not feel bound at all. The latter are able to explore inwardly their own horizons, their possibilities, and to feel creative. So it's not the role, or lifestyle, or choice which is inhibiting. It is the degree to which we subscribe to it as our total reality.

CT: So the same roles can be bondage for one and a feature of an expansive life view for another. The shift of attitude is to break through the idea of a role as the only reality.

CF: The primary factor is a sense of vision, both inner and outer. If there is no inner connection then the outer becomes all important; the role, functions, positions, jobs and chores become all consuming. It serves a purpose because it provides a sense of identity and a sense of being needed. If there is an inner connection, the outer doesn't have that emphasis. The role is part of one's life but not the whole of it. We can make our inner life visible in the world. Being a mother can be a strong and direct way of being present and effective in the world.

CT: Being identified with a role can be exhausting.

CF: Inevitably. If there is no inner connection then many women feel a vast sense of emptiness and loss; an interminable grief when their role becomes redundant. There seems to be nothing left that will make them somebody in the world. What is left is the feeling of being nothing.

CT: Isn't it the same for those who put so much emphasis on career?

CF: Yes. It depends how you use your outer life – whether you use it as a slot to lose yourself in or whether it is an outer manifestation of your inner awareness. With inner awareness you constantly undergo change. Therefore, your outer life offers up all manner of possibilities so you're never dependent on career, role or possession. There are certain things which contribute to change. But I don't think they are particularly specific to women. Often the factor is crisis. This can come about with loss – loss either through death or rejection, or loss of function or identity. For others, it is a feeling of inner discontent which cannot be ignored any longer. One may stay with an environment where everything seems superficially comfortable and smooth but inwardly one is unfulfilled. Something is missing. For others, it is the inner vision of an intuition of one's potential as a woman.

CT: How do you see this awakening of women in its historical perspective?

CF: I think it is often inspired by social reality. Just twenty years ago in the West, a woman's place was ordained from the time she was born – to be a wife, a mother and perhaps have a little job on the side. In the 1970s all that was questioned. Women were then thrown into a new identity crisis, again mostly by outer authorities, and those roles were no longer satisfactory. New expectations were placed on women to be feminist, independent and strong. This forced countless women into examining their relationship to life and to themselves.

Now the social expectations have changed again. Women are expected to be superwomen. We are expected to pursue a career, be professional, be financially stable and independent. We should also be good mothers, run good households and be very competent. It is a combination of the two past expectations. This new identity creates an enormous amount of pressure on women. Women still have to question who they are because of these major changes in expectations in the last thirty years. We have to question who we are very deeply and where we are going in our lives.

CT: Who is setting these standards?

CF: Magazines, books, movies, the media. Who wins the awards for being 'Woman of the Year'? The women we see on television are viewed with admiration. Our models are always set up by the input we receive. Ordinary women are constantly being questioned about whether they feel satisfied or dissatisfied with their lives. Women are being forced to keep looking. They must have the space for inner inquiry and questioning. The face of the ideal woman stares at us all the time. She makes only false and empty promises. She is not a friend to any woman. I can say that to any woman and she'll know exactly what I mean.

CT: What is the impact of that? I was in the newsagent's today and there must have been two complete shelves of women's magazines, each one having a very attractive woman filling the cover.

CF: I ask women, 'How many hours during your lifetime do you think you have spent looking in the mirror? Why do you do it?' For most women it is thousands and thousands and thousands of hours. It's not looking in the mirror simply because the mirror reflects back the image. It's looking in the mirror for the ideal woman. Do I have the right kind of face? Do I have the right kind of haircut? Do I have the right appearance? Do I have the right weight? In the number of collective hours we have spent looking in the mirror, we could have changed the world. We could have changed the whole world with that energy! Most of that energy has been undermining because perhaps only 0.0001 per cent find the face of the ideal woman in the mirror.

CT: Even those who are regarded socially as beautiful often do not think or feel that they are beautiful.

CF: There's always insecurity, always somebody more beautiful. No one can defend themselves against crows feet, wrinkles and excess fat. No one can defend themselves against their bodies and time. This enormous pressure on women can be useful and not negative when we find ourselves questioning our place in the world. So instead of blindly pursuing culturally accepted role models, women can ask themselves, 'Do I want to live like that? Do I want to get hormone injections to have full breasts? Do I want to dress like a man in order to appear professional?'

CT: Are you saying that the more blatant and crude the message of how women should be is, the more likelihood there is of women rebelling?

CF: Women are realizing that imitation of models is not a worthy pursuit. It is not the path to acceptability, worthiness or fulfilment. Women are caught up in the negative effects because their conditioning is so much orientated around being acceptable and approved of.

CT: What is going to make the shift from imitation of the so-called 'successful woman?'

CF: Women who are successful must question the goodies they get from being successful. Successful women get involved in playing the presentation game. They want to show the attributes of success. On a retreat I ask the women, 'How many images do you have about me? Do you expect me to fulfil them? Are you going to model yourself after them?'

CT: Don't we need role models?

CF: We do. But we need role models that are based on actuality, not based on fantasy. It's no good to emulate someone because they seem to have power, authority, control or spiritual achievements. It is worthwhile to emulate someone if that person encourages you to a find a truth about yourself, not to conform or copy what they are.

CT: It is interesting that we do not hear much about the inner feelings and day-to-day experiences of famous role models. Actually we have no idea what their inner life is like.

CF: Women who come on retreats express appreciation for having a woman teacher. It is valuable to have a few role models but I feel women are very fortunate in having very few authentic role models. If you do not have a model there is no one to tell you this is the proper way to do this, to tell you to do it this way to get a reward or tell you to follow this way to make progress. Without a model anywhere you have an enormous amount of freedom. You have nowhere to turn, except inwardly. You have no one to say to you, 'You're right. You're wrong. You're really progressing. You're doing badly.' Then praise and blame from another doesn't really matter. It takes an enormous amount of courage to let go of the outer authority. In many, many ways, it is a very free place to be.

CT: This is obviously contrary to the conventional wisdom. Conventional wisdom says, follow the model. By not having a model it is immediately freeing and liberating. But does it contribute to a liberated feeling inside?

CF: Not necessarily. Women have to call on their inner qualities. We have to be willing to accept our failures and mistakes. We cannot assume standpoints. If you have no clearly defined path you are at times going to adopt paths that lead to a dead end. It's very necessary to have the humility to say, 'I was wrong,' and to start again. It takes an enormous willingness not to assume any standpoints of, 'I know' or 'I am' or 'I have.' You have to be incredibly wary of such concepts. You have to be willing to listen to the feedback of others. It is a hard path for many women, I feel. But women are forming a vision of life which is enormously strengthening and empowering. Underneath their negative conditioning, women connect with life, as they spend time being with themselves and with each other. What I hear from women time and time again is a deep experience and vision of interconnectedness and oneness. If women listen to that and hearken to that then we don't make so many mistakes.

CT: In other words to realize interconnectedness is liberating.

CF: Yes. That is what I hear echoed from almost all women. And they know what comes from that is trust and wisdom. The process has its own momentum and is very organic. It's immediately very liberating. It's the source of women's empowerment, which discards negative conditioning. For hundreds of years spirituality has been at the root of women's vision. It's nothing new. Women have spoken of this realization and vision for generations upon generations. Yet it's totally new for women who discover it, a replica of what women have seen before.

Women have an enormous spiritual heritage that has survived every other single tradition. It has never been erased or modified by any tradition, whether Buddhist, Christian, Pagan or whatever. The same vision has continued despite the differences in conditioning, lifestyles and externals. In this seeing, women speak with the same voice.

CT: Women's realization of freedom and interconnectedness has widespread ramifications for social, religious and political realities.

CF: The process is escalating, although its implications have hardly begun to be felt. I feel it is a process from which there is no turning back. It is going to transform every level of our world. I feel the awakening of women is going to change everything.

The sensitized mind

An Interview with Roger Walsh
Santa Rosa, California

Dr Roger Walsh is a professor in the Department of Psychiatry and Human Behaviour at the University of California in Irvine. In 1981 he made a trip for several months to Burma and Thailand to practise meditation. The experience 'shook the solid foundation of his life,' and he learned in no uncertain terms that our ways of living in the world are not in tune with the global reality.

In his book *Staying Alive*, which received a nomination as political book of the year in the US, he wrote, 'Standing on a street corner [in Burma] for an hour, I learned as much about diseases and leprosy, congenital deformities and tuberculosis of the spine as I had learned in medical school. The tragedy was that the diseases were treatable, if only adequate medical resources were available.' The book deals with the psychology of human survival – with the state of the mind, the state of the world and the healing of the planet. It was an outcome of his observations and experiences in the East.

He goes on to say, 'The amount of preventable suffering was staggering. Overpopulation, poverty, malnutrition, pollution, disease; all were wreaking an extraordinary and unnecessary amount of pain.'

In the preface to his book, he writes, 'How could I have been so asleep? How could I have repressed the extent of preventable pain.' After he returned to California, where he has lived for the past fifteen years, he experienced a profound culture shock. So many activities 'seemed to aim at a continuous distraction away from deeper, more important concerns.'

For several years in a row, Roger has flown from the west coast of the US to the Insight Meditation Society in Barre, Massachusetts to participate in at least a portion of the three-month retreat there, generally attended by ninety people or more. Roger told me that for years his experiences with insight meditation were characterized by pain and difficulty, yet they persistently challenged his basic beliefs and assumptions about himself and who he was. Being challenged in this way made the pain of the process workable and it has only been recently that spiritual joy and the taste of bliss have been accessible during deep meditation.

Through his own experiencing, Roger realizes that discovering the vast hidden potential of the mind through the variety of religious forms and experiences available in the many religious traditions has a direct connection with the genuine well-being of both ourselves and the planet.

In this respect Roger's inner exploration directly influences his outer concerns because, as he points out, the problems are both 'out there' and 'in here'.

The interview was held at Santa Rosa, an hour's drive north of San Francisco where time was taken out during a ten-day retreat. His experiences, knowledge and sustained interest to learn and inquire brings from us who have contact with him an abiding affection and respect. So often an individual who is regarded as having reached a prestigious position within society tends to rest on their laurels. In Roger's case, however, his investigations into his inner world, combined with his knowledge of philosophy, psychology, religion and global realities, have led to sustained contributions, through his writings and his participation at conferences, to increasing public awareness about life on earth.

He is co-editor of *Beyond Ego* and *Beyond Health and Normality*. He has written numerous articles for the *American Journal of Psychiatry* and the *Journal of Humanistic Psychology*. His writings have received over a dozen national and international awards. And he deserves everyone of them. He is married to Frances Vaughan, a professor at the California Institute of Transpersonal Psychology.

CT: In your book *Staying Alive*, you refer to the problems of the planet as having their roots in psychological factors, including greed, aggression and ignorance. This implies the necessity to look both inwardly and outwardly at ourselves and the world. What part does religion have to play in facing the issues of the planet?

RW: I think it can play a crucial part because we are at a new phase in human history. For the first time, our technological power and our capacity to change the world are so great that the state of the world mirrors the state of our individual and collective minds. We look out at the world and what we see are the psychological forces and conflicts within us and between us mirrored back to us. What we see, therefore, are our *own* psychological and spiritual conflicts, distortions, and deficiencies reflected as the world's problems of our time.

Now, classically, religions have, at least in their higher or mystical forms provided us with pathways for training the mind to reduce intra- and interpersonal conflict. Through these methods, the emotions which create conflict, such as hatred and greed, are transformed into more socially beneficial emotions and behaviours such as love, compassion and joy for another's well-being. Psychology also aims at helping us to reduce negative qualities and cultivate the positive in the mind. At this time in history, religion and psychology may have increasingly more important roles to play, not only in individual well-being but also in our social and collective well-being.

CT: Sometimes the association with religion is nothing much more than ritual, a strong belief system, and possibly fundamentalism, which some people feel is distant from global reality.

RW: That is a very important point and indeed I'm using the term in a very specific way, which I should explain. I'm not referring so much to the popular rituals and beliefs which are so often mistaken for the totality of religious possibility and I'm certainly not referring to the rigid dogmas which have been the source of so much conflict and suffering. Rather, I'm pointing to something which is only now starting to become well known, and that is the common core of contemplative practices and wisdom found at the heart of all the great religions. This common core is sometimes known as the 'perennial wisdom' or 'perennial philosophy'.

What is notable about the perennial wisdom is that it emphasizes the importance of contemplative practices to train and change the mind. For centuries diverse religions have claimed that these practices – for example, meditation, yoga and contemplation – are capable of accelerating personal and spiritual development. The interesting thing is that recent psychological research is beginning to support these claims. People who practise such disciplines tend to be both psychologically and physically healthier, and to live lives of less consumption and of greater voluntary simplicity; they are probably more socially concerned, and even seem to live longer. I suspect that if these practices become more widespread they may help us live more sensitively and respond more appropriately to our current global problems. On the other hand, there's the very real danger that religious fanaticism may prevail and exacerbate our problems. Throughout human history countless millions of people have died because of their belief that 'mine is the only true way'. But with the kinds of weapons now at our disposal such beliefs may be suicidal, perhaps even omnicidal. How religions are understood and practised may help determine the fate of our species.

CT: A person may say that these various spiritual disciplines and practices are a life-long task. Meanwhile, the planet is facing global extinction.

RW: That is a classical dilemma. The question is, to what extent should we work on ourselves and to what extent should we direct our efforts to other people and the outer world? It is interesting that we tend to think of this question in extremes – that we must do one or the other. Yet in point of fact, if one looks at history, one finds an interesting phenomenon which the great historian Arnold Toynbee called 'the cycle of withdrawal and return'. What he found was that those people who had contributed most to human development and well-being throughout history exhibited a common life pattern. First, they withdrew from society for a while to go inward to confront their questions and fears and to wrestle with the basic questions of human existence. Having come to some understanding they then returned with that wisdom to share it with other people, having become, in the process, more effective instruments of service. Often they exhibited this cycle of withdrawal and return several times during the course of their lives.

So it is important to see that one does not need to do only one or the other, but to see that one may cycle through these two phases of inner and outer work. Of course, it is also possible to combine them so that one goes out into the world not only to heal and serve, but also to learn and awaken oneself and others in the process. Going out into the world then leads one deeper into oneself. In the East this has been known as 'karma yoga', the yoga of service and work in the world. In the West, it has been known as service and learning. There doesn't have to be the sharp distinction between serving others and enhancing one's own well-being. The two may eventually merge.

CT: In the West, would you say that a contemporary example of 'withdrawal and return' would be people going into retreats, or workshops, for renewal and then going back into daily life?

RW: Yes, certainly. And I think we are seeing greater numbers of people doing that and seeing more products of that. In fact, my book, *Staying Alive: The Psychology of Human Survival*, was a result of this process. There is no way that I could have written the book without the inspiration that retreats gave me.

CT: What kind of influence, if any, is this having on our major institutions – the established churches, the field of politics, medicine, science, education?

RW: My own feeling about this is that there are some inroads being made but that, as yet, they are still quite small. In the last decade, traditional churches have shown a dramatic resurgence of interest in contemplation. In education, there are clearly some effects, though again small. There is an increasing number of courses being given in religious studies and on the psychology of the contemplative traditions. There is a whole new area of psychology called 'transpersonal psychology', which studies those states of consciousness in which there is an experience of the sense of self expanding beyond (*trans*) the usual personality or ego limits. Some of these transpersonal states have been regarded historically as the *summum bonum* or highest goal of human existence by several religions.

This attempt by psychologists to understand what were once thought of as purely religious phenomena is beginning to expand our understanding of human development. To give an example of the impact that it is having: within the last decade, Western psychologists have dramatically increased their exploration of adult development. Especially in mature and psychologically healthy people, the upper levels of psychological development seem to look suspiciously like the early stages of spiritual development. In the last few years, we have begun to see the first full spectrum models of development which trace human psychological development from infancy through normal adulthood and then beyond, into various spiritual stages and even into levels of enlightenment.

CT: How would you describe the difference between a psychologically healthy human being and one who is living with spiritual insights and awareness?

RW: First, we have to appreciate that there is considerable overlap. A psychologically healthy person is one who experiences a minimum of conflict and defensiveness. There are considerable data to show that this type of person is one who tends to be altruistic and generous, and derives great satisfaction from the process of giving of themselves. It is interesting to look at that and see that these are characteristics that are classically descriptive of religious development and maturity. A person who has a degree of spiritual insight and understanding might have access to a range of altered states of consciousness. He or she might have a deeper understanding of their self nature, or transpersonal nature, that is beyond the personality or the ego. That person might identify primarily with consciousness rather than with the body. He or she might sometimes experience a unitive state of consciousness in which there is compassion for all beings, not just one's friends or family, but all living beings. In such a state of mind, the sense of identity becomes increasingly encompassing with fewer dichotomies or distinction from other people.

CT: Both a psychologically healthy person and a spiritually conscious person often seem to show a definite resistance to being engaged in the troubles of the world.

RW: I think that can certainly happen but I wonder if this resistance hasn't been exaggerated in many cases. We hear so often that people concerned with self-actualization, self-growth, self-exploration, etc. are nothing but narcissictic and selfish. Now I'm sure that this *can* be the case, but I'm not sure it's always or even often the case. In fact, research shows clearly that psychologically healthy and mature people tend to be more altruistic and socially concerned than other people. But, as you say, some individuals involved in psychological and spiritual growth work may not be particularly involved in immediate social or political contribution. But again, I don't think that we should rush to judge them. Some of them may indeed have become overly withdrawn from social involvement. On the other hand, for some of them it may be only a temporary phase before they find themselves drawn to share whatever they've learned. Another positive interpretation is that some people feel that their greatest contributions may come from changing and healing minds, including their own, rather than working on specific projects or things in the world.

CT: There is certainly value to that viewpoint.

RW: That viewpoint gains increasing credence if we recognize, as I think we are forced to, that the state of the world today really does reflect our state of mind. Also, there seems to be a developmental process that people in spiritual practice go through. First, they become increasingly sensitized to their experience, both inner and outer. Then they find themselves less and less able to keep out the pain and suffering of the world and more and more sensitive to the cries for help that pour forth from every television screen and every quarter of the globe. An enormous, indeed incomprehensible, amount of suffering surrounds us. Someone with a sensitized mind is increasingly pulled to work to alleviate this suffering in whatever ways that he or she can. I find that as I go around and speak to people about the state of the world what gives me hope is the growing number of people who are committing their lives to working with global issues. I find that very inspiring.

CT: What is your response when a person says, 'Well, what can I do except work on myself?'

RW: I think the first thing to realize is that this is not a simple question. Most of us, when we first awaken to the crises and suffering in the world, do so with an enormous sense of urgency. We think we should know immediately what is the best contribution we can make. We often fail to realize that this question is really one of the most profound and complex that we as individuals and humankind have ever faced. It may be very important to be patient and, at least for a while, be willing not to know what to do. In fact, not knowing may be part of the answer. If we look around the world we find that a lot of the world's problems are caused by people who think that they know what the answers are and then impose their answers on others.

CT: The first step, then, is not knowing and retaining the question.

RW: Exactly. We need to realize that the question, 'How can I best contribute to healing our global crisis?' is not something we answer overnight. For me it took almost two years from the time of recognizing how urgent the world situation is until I could see that I might be able to contribute through working on the psychology of human survival. Taking time can be very important. Let it be OK not to know. We really crucify ourselves with 'the tyranny of shoulds'. We have the idea that we should be able to come up with answers immediately. Precipitous action may not be helpful. Reflective action is much more likely to be strategic.

CT: What comes next?

RW: The second thing which I think is important for us to do is to take some time to educate ourselves. This education has to be of two types. First, it has to be about the state of the world and the problems we are facing so we can act with awareness and respond in a strategic way. The second type of education we need is about the psychological and spiritual causes which have created the problems in the first place so that we can act with understanding. The famous English author, H. G. Wells, said, 'History becomes increasingly a race between education and catastrophe.' So education of both ourselves and others is crucial.

The third step is not only to look at the question of what I can do but what I truly want to do. We are most likely to be effective if the work we are doing is a path of the heart and consistent with our deeper wishes. True contribution doesn't have to be a sacrifice. Most of us have the idea that it is. That can be a very self-destructive idea.

CT: Why is that?

RW: Firstly, it leads to burnout because we are acting out of 'shoulds' instead of 'wants'. Secondly, it leads to resentment and anger which, of course, takes the joy out of the whole process. Yet what we are trying to do is to increase joy and reduce suffering. It's not likely to be helpful if we work in ways which create more suffering.

The fourth step in social–global contribution is to look for groups of like-minded people. There is strength in numbers. One of the things which I find most encouraging is the increase in the number of globally-oriented groups in the last few years. I recently looked up *The Encylopaedia of Organizations* in the United States and found that half the globally-concerned groups here had been formed within the last five years. I find that very encouraging.

CT: Very encouraging! Are there other considerations for action?

RW: The fifth thing, I think, is to play a kind of game with ourselves. It is not only to ask what I can do but what is the most strategic thing I can do. We can look at optimizing our impact, using the inspirational examples of people like Mother Teresa or Gandhi. We tend to think of these people as spiritual geniuses who could automatically come up with marvellous ideas and solutions. But if we look carefully at their lives, we find they often spent long periods in contemplation, prayer and reflection, seeking inspiration as to what would be the most strategic contributions that they could make. The game we could play might be: 'If Mother Teresa or Mahatma Gandhi were living *my* life with *my* friends, skills and connections, what would they do?'

CT: This means applying fantasy and visualization prior to action as well as contemplation and reflection.

RW: It is certainly important to take time for one's own inner work and remember the value of withdrawal and return; to take time to go within, to rediscover one's emotional, psychological and spiritual nourishment whether by being in nature, in a retreat, or with supportive people.

CT: When we put all these points together, it contributes in a real way to being effective inwardly and outwardly. Some people tell me there are so many issues they don't know what to turn to. It seems our society takes up hot off the press issues like child abuse, drugs, alcohol, poverty, South Africa, crime, famine, Nicaragua, AIDS, nuclear weapons, the arms trade, the forests. There is a tremendous burst of public interest and then the issue is forgotten because a new issue, a new crisis, has arisen. How does one sustain commitment in spite of the hype which goes up and down in waves of newsprint?

RW: It sounds like you are asking two questions. One is how to choose an issue and second, how to maintain dedication to it? Ultimately, we can only trust our own sense of what seems right for us to do because there are no hard and fast rules that speak to our unique situation. Only we can know when it is appropriate to stay with an issue and when it is appropriate to change. However, perhaps one can work across a wider range of problems by appreciating that the fundamental causes of our collective problems are not purely military, economic and political, but also psychological and spiritual. To the extent that one is working on these deeper dimensions both within oneself and the world, one is working not only on the so-called problems (which are actually symptoms) but also the underlying causes.

CT: This is where the interfacing of ourselves and totality becomes so important because our heart and minds are connected to the world.

RW: There's considerable data emerging from psychology showing that service contributes to psychological and presumably, also spiritual well-being, as the sages have claimed across history. I think there may be a fundamental error within the assumption that we have to be completely integrated and enlightened before we can serve.

CT: You live and work in California. A growing number of people here use the invaluable resources of psychotherapy and meditation. But in many places in the West people think, 'I'm not neurotic. I don't need a therapist.'

RW: I think you're right. In much of the world, psychotherapy is only used for the seriously disturbed. As yet there is little appreciation that therapy and meditation can enhance well-being in normal people and also make them more willing and able to be helpful to others and be socially involved.

CT: Doesn't consumerism hinder human beings from being in touch with important social and existential questions?

RW: I think it more than hinders. I think it is actually a defence mechanism against the recognition of these issues. Consumerism and the insatiable demand for ever more stimulation and gratification through money, power, drugs, sex, food and possessions can actually be substitute gratifications for higher needs. What is little known in our culture is that when the desire for truth, realization and transcendence is not acknowledged within oneself, it results in types of pathology – like cynicism, alienation, meaninglessness or addiction. Not knowing that this is an existential pathology and not knowing how to deal with it, the mind turns to the old gratifications. But since these gratifications are not what we really need and since we can never get enough of what we don't really need, we end up in a vicious cycle of compulsively consuming more and more yet feeling fundamentally unsatisfied.

CT: The dominant religion of our time is consumerism, with the supermarket as the local church or synagogue where various items are worshipped on the altar.

RW: What is also not acknowledged is that the addiction to consumption is actually just that – an addiction. One then needs increasing amounts for one's fix – whether the fix be possessions, power, status or sex – in order to get the same results.

CT: There is some public awareness about the addiction of alcohol and drugs but little about consumerism.

RW: One of the important things that Asian wisdom traditions have to teach us is that we can become addicted to anything, internal or external. Society has not yet appreciated that and we and our planet are suffering greatly because of it.

Christopher Titmuss is a member of:

Action on Smoking and Health (ASH), 5–11 Mortimer Street, London W1N 7RH.

Amnesty International, 5 Roberts Place, off Bowling Green Lane, London EC1R 0EJ.

Animal Aid, 7 Castle Street, Tonbridge, Kent.

Buddhist Peace Fellowship, 8 West Allington, Bridport, Dorset, DT6 5BG.

Campaign for Nuclear Disarmament (CND), 22 Underwood Street, London N1 7JG.

Friends of the Earth, 26 Underwood Street, London N1 7JQ.

Green Party, 10 Station Parade, Balham High Road, London SW12 9AZ.

Greenpeace, 30–31 Islington Green, London N1 8XE.

Insight Meditation Society, Barre, Massachusetts 01005, USA.

Oxfam (Oxford Committee for Famine Relief), 274 Banbury Road, Oxford OX2 7DZ.

Schumacher Society, Ford House, Hartland, Bideford, Devon EX39 6EE.

Survival International, 310 Edgware Road, London W2 1DY.

Vegetarian Society, Parkdale, Cheshire WA14 4QG.

War on Want, 37 Great Guildford Street, London SE1.

More paperbacks from

Green Print

The books described on the following pages can be ordered from all competent booksellers. Many bookshops have them in stock. For our current catalogue and to join our free mailing list, write to Green Print, The Merlin Press, 10 Malden Road, London NW5 3HR.

Teaching Green

A parent's guide to education for life on Earth

Damian Randle

The world is going green. But is education keeping up? Parents and teachers must work together to make sure it does. Teaching Green points the way.

Green education will help children to grow as fulfilled, independent and caring people – active democrats co-operating with each other and with the earth. Simple in style, radical in content and outspoken in tone, this book guides parents, teachers and students towards an education that is good for people and good for the earth.

It emphasises emotional, spiritual and physical, as well as intellectual, needs. It stresses the need for children and young people to learn to work together, not against one another. And it uncovers ways of developing technologies, lifestyles and political practices which will enable us to sustain life on earth beyond the current phase of rapacious, anti-ecological industrialism.·

Damian Randle shares with the reader the many insights gained by people who are already pioneering new ideas and new techniques. The book is packed with examples of new education in action, and is an inspiration to the rapidly growing number of parents and teachers dissatisfied with education as presently understood.

The author was a teacher for twelve years before becoming joint education officer at the Centre for Alternative Technology, Machynlleth. His last post was as head of faculty at a Community High School near Wolverhampton. He is editor of Green Teacher, an international journal for teachers and educators which he founded in 1986.

The Stolen Future

How to rescue the Earth for our Children

Patrick Rivers

The environment crisis now making headlines is no surprise. Entirely predictable, ignored despite warnings from countless eminent authorities, it has been brewing for aeons: only the timing lay in doubt. For as human beings we suffer from crucial defects built into our nature, and a resultant collective lunacy is now climaxing. By stealing from our children the very future they expect and deserve, we risk becoming just one more endangered species.

The measures that politicians are now hastily assembling amount to little more than delaying tactics. Remedies have to reach root causes. As individuals and as a species we must first acknowledge our unflattering limitations and identify our buried qualities. And then make a pact with the planet on which we totally depend. In short, unless we put Earth first we cannot last.

These are some of the many contentious findings in this well-timed book. Patrick Rivers asks 'If we ignore such a challenge, how can we look our children in the eyes and declare we love them above all else?'.

Tracing the course of human history, he depicts how we have let a male-dominated, over-industrialised society, and the values that go with it, warp our true nature so severely that we have become a species under pandemic stress. Like laboratory rats or caged animals, our behaviour has become freakish and obsessive. As our power has outstripped our sense of responsibility, we have so lost sight of vital connections that we have let world crisis engulf us.

To escape extinction we need to re-create societies where we can regain touch with our roots. Only then can we replace our media-reinforced self-image of a competitive, ruthless and selfish species with one of co-operation, trust, compassion and selfish species with one of co-operation, trust, compassion and tolerance. By replacing exploitation with renewal our needs and those of the planet can be reconciled.

'Absolutely excellent. If only every literate person in the Western world would read it.' – John Seymour.

'An important book which goes wider and deeper than most green books in considering the causes and solutions of the crises facing mankind.' – Clive Ponting.

The Race for Riches

Jeremy Seabrook

With extraordinary passion and insight, Jeremy Seabrook interweaves the techniques of novel, documentary and polemic to lay bare the myths of modern economics and the empty values which underpin our society. We see the reality of today's world manifested in the lives of ordinary people everywhere, be they in London, Wales, or India. He gives the lie to a myth of progress which offers people an illusion of relief from poverty – a poverty which, instead of being transformed into sufficiency, is deftly turned into another form of privation. The constant factor is the multiple and varied way in which humanity is wasted in this malign project. Everywhere we find the same promise of relief from insecurity and scarcity: yet the reality is always immiseration.

Such development can never emancipate. It can change the nature of poverty, but can never free people from it. Even the richest have a desperate urgency to acquire which has nothing to do with human need, but instead is part of a soulless system which we inhabit and which animates us. We can no longer distinguish between our own hunger for possessions, and that system's insatiable search for profit. There is in fact no problem of poverty – or there would not be, but for the far more intractable problem of wealth and its abusive and monopolistic control of the necessities of the poor.

We must puncture the pretensions of the rich: we must de-mystify wealth, and remove its sacred aura. Our objective: the green project of a satisfying plenty for all. The race for riches by passes the more modest and achievable goal of sufficiency, and leads only to mutations of poverty: to loss, dependency, insecurity. The only cure is a liberation into a sustainable harmony with the Earth that bears us all.

This book is about that race, and that cure.

Living Without Cruelty

Mark Gold

Recipes by Sarah Brown

'Living without Cruelty', 'Beauty Without Cruelty' and the 'Cruelty-Free' consumer campaign are three national campaigns run by the major animal welfare and vegetarian pressure groups and charities. This book encapsulates the arguments of all these campaigns.

The book argues with passion for a commitment to a cruelty-free lifestyle as part of a commitment to a radical green awareness. Mark Gold shows how our everyday living can have cruel and often unforeseen consequences for animals and humans alike. Topics covered include animal suffering, human health, vivisection, entertainment, pets and clothing.

The conclusions are positive and up-beat. The author emphasises the practical alternatives that are available to us in our daily lifestyle – in the kitchen, around the house, the ways we bring up our children, and so on. The book features product listings and a resource guide.

TV cook SARAH BROWN has contributed a collection of original recipes, helping the reader to put theory into delicious practice on the meal table.

'A handy guide to animal welfare and the personal routes a consumer or campaigner can take to the business of living without cruetly' – Richard North, The Independent.

'Real food for thought' – Daily Telegraph.

'This helpful book powerfully explains how our lives are interrelated with animals, how we share a common planet' – Colin Spencer.

'Just what we have all been waiting for' – The Vegetarian.